Martin and the brigands.   The Cloisters Collection.   (PLATE VII)

The St. Martin Embroideries

A fifteenth-century
series illustrating
the life and legend
of St. Martin of Tours

MARGARET B. FREEMAN
CURATOR EMERITUS OF THE CLOISTERS

THE METROPOLITAN MUSEUM OF ART

DISTRIBUTED BY NEW YORK GRAPHIC SOCIETY LTD., Greenwich, Connecticut

Contents

Acknowledgments

Many people have helped in the preparation of this study, and I would like to thank each one. First, I wish to express my appreciation to the owners and custodians of the embroideries, both past and present, who have cooperated so graciously and generously, with considerable interest in the project: Robert de Machaux, Director of the Musée Historique des Tissus in Lyons; Robert Lehman and the curator of his collection, George Szabo; Alastair Bradley Martin; the Cooper Union Museum and Judge Irwin Untermyer; the Walters Art Gallery; Countess Margit Batthyany; and Mrs. Ernest Brummer. I am grateful to Charles Sterling for reviewing with me the style of the roundels; to Colin Eisler for bringing to my attention the embroidery in Ghent; to Donald King, Deputy Keeper of Textiles in the Victoria and Albert Museum, for informing me of the 1887 photograph; and to Harry Bober for giving me several pertinent suggestions. I also wish to thank my colleagues in the Metropolitan for their considerable help, criticism, and encouragement: Thomas P. F. Hoving, William H. Forsyth, Edith A. Standen, Vera K. Ostoia, Bonnie Young, Thomas P. Miller, and most especially Carmen Gómez-Moreno.

M.B.F.

The St. Martin
Embroideries

INTRODUCTION

IN THE MIDDLE AGES people liked their embroidered textiles not only beautiful, with shining gold and silken threads, but also meaningful, with scenes from well-loved stories of saints and heroes. The tale of Tristan and Isolde, for instance, would be stitched on a bedspread, and the life of Christ on a liturgical cope. Pictorial embroidery was, in every sense of the phrase, a fine art, and those who made pictures with needle and thread were often as highly skilled and as highly valued as those who made pictures with brush and pigment. Their work was known as needle painting (*peinture à l'aiguille*).

In 1947 four small fifteenth-century needle paintings of high quality were acquired for the Treasury at The Cloisters from the estate of Joseph Brummer. At the time they were purchased almost nothing was known about them except that they had been bought by Mr. Brummer from a dealer in Italy. Their country of origin and their date were matters of dispute, and the subjects of the scenes were a mystery. In June 1955 two of the embroideries were published in the Museum's *Bulletin,* in an article entitled "The Legend of Saint Catherine told in Embroidery." In this article it was noted that although the four embroideries are of the same shape (round) and about the same size (six and a half inches in diameter), they belong to two separate series, distinct in drawing, color range, technique, and iconography. It was established that two of them were once part of a large ensemble illustrating the story of St. Catherine, of which eight roundels are known to exist today. They were compared in style to the early work of Rogier van der Weyden and his associates and were dated about 1440.

After several years of study, it is now possible to report the results of research on the other two Cloisters roundels. They are closely related to thirty other roundels. Eight of these were also in the Brummer collection, and are now dispersed in the United States: four in the collection of Robert Lehman, New York City, two in the Cooper Union Museum, New York City, one in the Walters Art Gallery, Baltimore, and one in the collection of Alastair Bradley Martin, Guennol, Long Island. Twenty-two roundels, the larger part of the series, are in the Musée Historique des Tissus in Lyons, France, mounted in a seventeenth-century setting as orphreys for chasubles, crosses for the backs and vertical strips for the fronts (*Figures 1–4*).

In addition to the thirty-two roundels, there are four embroideries in the shape of arched panels and one embroidery, oval in form, that relate to the roundels in iconography though they differ in technique of stitchery and style of drawing. Two of the panels are the centers of the chasuble crosses in Lyons. A third is in the collection of Countess Margit Batthyany, Castagnola, Switzerland. A photograph dated 1887, discovered in 1955 by Donald King, Deputy Keeper of Textiles of the Victoria and Albert Museum, shows this panel and seven of the Brummer roundels in a seventeenth-century arrangement similar to that of the Lyons embroideries (*Figure 5*). One of the roundels in this photograph belongs to the St. Catherine series, published as noted above; the others are part of the ensemble that is the subject of this study. The fourth panel has been for many years on exhibition at The Cloisters, as a generous loan from Alastair Bradley Martin. It, too, was once part of a chasuble cross, as is shown by an undated and unlabeled photograph found in December 1967 by Mrs. Ernest Brummer among Brummer records in a warehouse (*Figure 6*). Along with the panel are five St. Catherine roundels, including the one in the 1887 photograph, and one roundel that belongs to the series under discussion here. The oval embroidery is on the hood of a cope in the church of St. Michael in Ghent (*Figure 7*). Because of the significant differences in style and technique, the arched panels and the oval will be discussed after the roundels. All of the embroideries, illustrated as PLATES I– XXXVII, are reproduced at facsimile size, as near as can be determined.

The Lyons embroideries were published by Louis de Farcy in 1919 in his *La Broderie du XIe siècle jusqu'à nos jours*.[1] Here he states: ". . . these beautiful and fine embroideries at one time composed altar frontals (*fronteaux*), consecrated to the life of different saints. . . . They were mutilated in the seventeenth century to make into chasubles. M. Duponchel, a dealer, possesses two almost the same, having undergone the same transformation, probably in a convent in Arras."

Neither de Farcy nor the authorities of the Lyons museum identified

Figure 1

Chasuble cross with seven roundels and one panel.

Musée Historique des Tissus, Lyons

Figure 2

Second chasuble cross with seven roundels and one panel.

Musée Historique des Tissus, Lyons

Figures 3, 4

Orphreys, each with four roundels.

Musée Historique des Tissus, Lyons

Figure 6

Chasuble cross with six roundels and one panel.

Photo courtesy Mrs. Ernest Brummer

the saint or "different saints" represented in the embroideries. It can now be shown that all of the thirty-two roundels, the four panels, and the oval illustrate scenes from the life and legend of St. Martin. Martin was born about 316 of pagan parents in the Roman province of Pannonia (now part of Hungary), and became bishop of Tours, beloved healer, worker of marvels, friend of the poor, apostle to the Gauls, and patron saint of France. Probably he was

Figure 8

St. Martin dividing his cloak with the beggar, from the *Hours* of the Maréchal de Boucicaut.

Musée Jacquemart-André, Paris, ms. 2, fol. 34 verso

not identified previously because not one of the embroideries illustrates the best-known, unmistakable episode of St. Martin dividing his cloak with the beggar (*Figure 8*).

It was one of the Lehman roundels that gave the clue to the interpretation of the whole series. This (PLATE XVII) shows a scene of a feast in which a nimbed bishop, a crowned king and queen, and a priest are being served by two green-garbed squires. The bishop is about to offer a golden cup to the priest. It seemed that this might be an incident in the life of St. Martin described by the thirteenth-century writer Jacobus da Voragine in *The Golden Legend*. St. Martin "was of such great humility," says Voragine, that when the emperor Maximian had bidden him to a feast and the wine cup was brought to Martin to drink, Martin passed the cup first to his priest instead of to the emperor, "for he wist well that there was none worthy to drink before the priest."[2]

With this clue it was possible to identify with certainty the scene in one of the Cloisters roundels (PLATE VII). Here, the young saint, in secular garments, is calmly lecturing to a band of armed ruffians. With a flamboyant gesture, one of the ruffians is about to sheathe his sword while a fat-faced, fat-bellied companion looks in the direction of the action but points the other way. As Voragine tells the story, it was soon after Martin's baptism that he was "warned of our Lord . . . that he should visit his father and mother," who were still pagans, in order to convert them. But as he went over the mountains into Italy where his parents were living at the time, he fell among thieves, who struck at him with an ax, bound him, and then asked him if he were not afraid. Martin answered by saying that he was sure of God's mercy; he began to preach to the chief of the brigands "and converted him to the faith of Jesus Christ, and then the thief brought Martin forth on his way and afterward lived a good life."[3]

Here, then, were two St. Martin scenes. A third, in the Cooper Union Museum (PLATE XXXI), was then recognized as one of the miracles performed by St. Martin after his death. There were two beggars, one lame and the other blind. The blind man carried the lame man, and the lame man showed the blind man the way. The pair were very successful at their begging. Now they heard that the body of St. Martin was to be carried from a certain church in procession through their town, and knowing that many sick men had been healed by the saintly relics, they fled toward a different part of town, for they had no wish to be cured and thus deprived of their easy and profitable profession. But, writes Voragine, "as they fled they encountered . . . the holy body suddenly, unpurveyed . . . and were both healed against their will, and were right sorry therefor."[4] Though worn, the embroidery brilliantly depicts a strong man stumbling hurriedly down a street, bearing on his back a figure with useless limbs and an anxious face, while around the corner appears the holy Martin "unpurveyed."

Another roundel in Lyons proved to be the sequel to the best-known incident in the life of St. Martin, the dividing of his cloak. While Martin was a young soldier in the service of the emperor Julian, writes Voragine, "in

18

The empress kneeling before Martin.   The Cloisters Collection.   (PLATE XVIII)

a winter time as he passed by the gate of Amiens, he met a poor man all naked, to whom no man gave alms. Then Martin drew out his sword and carved his mantle therewith in two pieces in the middle and gave . . . one half to the poor man, for he had nothing else to give him, and he clad himself with that other half." As was mentioned before, this distinctive episode is missing from the series. The Lyons embroidery (PLATE III) illustrates the conclusion of the story. Martin is in bed, and, above, Christ holds out the part of the mantle that Martin had given to the poor man. According to the legend, Christ appeared to Martin in a dream, wearing the half cloak, and he said to the angels that were about him, "Martin, yet new in the faith, hath covered me with this vesture."[5]

With these four roundels identified, one by one all the others were found to fit into the iconographic scheme. The life and legend of St. Martin can be found in many medieval sources. The most valuable is the volume including the *Vita sancti Martini, Epistolae,* and *Dialogi* by the scholar Sulpicius Severus[6] (about 363–425), a contemporary and good friend of Martin. The more than two hundred miracles performed at the saint's tomb in the basilica at Tours are described by the sixth-century Gregory of Tours in his *De virtutibus sancti Martini.*[7] Gregory's *Historia Francorum*[8] includes further information about St. Martin and his miracles. Several of the marvels attendant on the journey of St. Martin's relics through Burgundy and other parts of France when the Northmen were devastating the Loire Valley are related in the *Miracula beati Martini post reversionem . . .*[9] by an unknown author who claimed to be Herbernus, archbishop of Tours, and in the *De reversione beati Martini a Burgundia, Tractatus,*[10] wrongly attributed to Odo, abbot of Cluny. Both tracts were probably written in the twelfth century. Jacobus da Voragine, in the thirteenth century, drew upon these sources for his life of St. Martin in the *Golden Legend.* A large proportion of the incidents illustrated in the embroideries are described by Voragine, and his account "as Englished by William Caxton" is frequently quoted in this study.[11] Another thirteenth-century work that proved helpful was the poem *Vie de Monseigneur saint Martin* by Péan Gastineau, canon of St. Martin of Tours.[12]

ROUNDELS: ICONOGRAPHY

THE EMBROIDERIES comprise a remarkably extensive series depicting the life and legend of a single saint. The earliest episode in the life of St. Martin to be illustrated in the embroideries is shown in one of Mr. Lehman's roundels (PLATE I). Here Martin as a lad – Sulpicius Severus states that he was ten years of age[13]– announces to his parents and other members of the family, all of whom were pagans at the time, that he wishes to become a catechumen. Martin's determined stance, the perplexity of the man at the left, and the dismay of the man at the right indicate very well that Martin took this step "against the will of all his kin," as Voragine reports.

When Martin was fifteen, he was commanded to join the army of the emperor, and thus, says Voragine, he "was made a knight." Mr. Martin's roundel (PLATE II) shows the young saint on horseback saying farewell to his parents while the emperor himself in royal robes stands watching.

It was while Martin was in the army that he divided his mantle to give half of it to a poor man, and then in a dream saw Christ with the same half cloak (PLATE III). Soon after this event Martin decided to be baptized. One of the Cooper Union embroideries (PLATE IV) illustrates this occasion. Young Martin, waist-deep in water in a gilded baptismal font, clasps his hands while the officiating cleric laves his head, and another cleric, very alert, waits with opened book, presumably a Sacramentary.

"Then held he yet chivalry two years," according to Voragine. "And in the meanwhile the barbarians entered among the Frenchmen, and [the emperor] Julian . . . gave great money unto the knights. And Martin willing no more to fight refused his gift but said to Caesar: I am a knight of Jesu Christ, it pertaineth not to me for to fight. Then Julian was wroth, and said that it was not for the grace of religion that he renounced chivalry but for fear and dread of the present battle following. To whom Martin, not being afeard, said to him: Because that thou holdest it for cowardice and that I have not done it

PLATE I   Martin informing his family that he will become a Christian.

Collection of Robert Lehman, New York

PLATE II Martin bidding his parents farewell as he joins the emperor's army.

Collection of Alastair Bradley Martin, Guennol, Long Island

PLATE III   Christ appearing to Martin in a dream, with the half cloak.

Musée Historique des Tissus, Lyons

PLATE IV   Martin being baptized.

Cooper Union Museum, New York, gift of Irwin Untermyer

PLATE V   Martin refusing to fight.

Musée Historique des Tissus, Lyons

for good faith, I shall [go] to-morn all unarmed tofore the battle, and shall be protected and kept by the sign of the cross. . . . But on the morn the enemies sent messengers that they would yield them[selves] and their goods, whereof it is no doubt that by the merits of this holy man . . . this victory was had without shedding of blood." One of the roundels in Lyons (PLATE V) shows Martin refusing to fight. He kneels unarmed before the emperor, who is accompanied by four fully armed and accoutered "knights."

And so Martin departed from "chivalry" and thereafter devoted himself to the religious life. He went first to St. Hilaire, bishop of Poiters, who ordained him as exorcist, one of the minor orders of the church. This ceremony is represented in one of Mr. Lehman's roundels (PLATE VI). A bright-eyed St. Martin (whose halo has worn away), clad in alb and amice, genuflects before the altar while St. Hilaire, wearing his bishop's miter and a priest's chasuble, blesses his new exorcist.

The Cloisters roundel of Martin and the brigands, already discussed (PLATE VII), is the next in the series. Another of Mr. Lehman's embroideries follows (PLATE VIII). Here Martin, habited as a monk, makes the sign of blessing over a prostrate nude figure, with head thrown back, unmistakably dead. As the story is told by Sulpicius Severus,[14] Martin established himself in a hermitage near Poitiers. One day, returning from a journey, he found that a young man whom he was instructing in the Christian faith had died without baptism. Martin fell on his knees and prayed; as he prayed he felt the Divine Presence, and as he watched he saw the dead man move and come to life. It was the first of Martin's many miracles.

The fame of Martin soon spread abroad, and when the bishopric of Tours fell vacant the people demanded that Martin be chosen as their next bishop. Martin himself was reluctant, and several in the church hierarchy opposed his election. Among them was one who was called a "defensor." Now it happened that one day a man, substituting for the regular lector who was unable to push his way through the crowd, opened the Psalter at random and read a verse from the eighth Psalm including the words, according to Voragine: ". . . for thine enemies thou shalt destroy the enemy defensor." "And thus," continues Voragine, "that defensor was chased out of the town by all the people," and it was clear to all that it was God's will that Martin be made bishop of Tours. One of the Lyons roundels (PLATE IX) probably illustrates this

PLATE VI   Martin and St. Hilaire.

Collection of Robert Lehman, New York

PLATE VII   Martin and the brigands.

The Metropolitan Museum of Art, The Cloisters Collection, 47.101.64

event. Here the reader balances the open Psalter on a book cabinet while he glances meaningfully at the saint, who stands apart with hands joined in prayer.

Thus Martin was ordained bishop of Tours. As bishop he continued to heal the sick and help the poor. Several of these deeds of mercy are illustrated in the embroideries. In one (PLATE X) he is shown at the gates of a city kissing a leper, "horrible to all men," as Voragine says, and thereby making "him whole." Martin is garbed in the cloak of a traveler, and the leper wears a distinctive large-brimmed leper's hat and carries a clapper, used to warn people of his passing. The afflicted man's wasted face contrasts with the youthful health of Martin's. In another roundel (PLATE XI) Martin cures a man possessed of a demon. As Sulpicius Severus tells the story, Martin was entering a house when he stopped at the threshold saying that he had just seen a frightful demon in the atrium. Martin ordered the demon to go away, but instead it entered the body of the father of the household, who immediately bit himself furiously and tore at all who came near him. There was "alarm in the house, distraction among the slaves, terrified flight of the population!" Martin flung himself in front of the demoniac and forced his fingers into his mouth, saying, "Eat them if you can." The man possessed opened his jaws lest he bite the fingers of the holy Martin, and the demon fled from his body.[15] The embroidery shows Martin about to thrust his fingers into the mouth of the unfortunate man, who does indeed appear to be demented.

The slave of a certain proconsul named Taedradius was also possessed of an evil spirit. According to Sulpicius Severus, although his proconsul fell on his knees before Martin, begging him to come and heal the sufferer, Martin refused, declaring that "he could not enter the house of a profane person, a pagan." Then Taedradius promised that if Martin would drive out the demon he himself would become a Christian. Martin placed his hands on the slave, who was immediately freed of "the unclean spirit," and Taedradius thereafter "believed in Jesus Christ."[16] This miracle is probably the subject of the embroidery (PLATE XII) that shows a richly dressed gentleman on his knees before St. Martin, while behind him a rather sick-looking figure reclines by the windows of a little house.

Another roundel in Lyons (PLATE XIII) partially illustrates a second occasion when Martin clothed a poor man. He commanded his archdeacon

PLATE VIII   Martin brings to life a dead man.

Collection of Robert Lehman, New York

PLATE IX   Martin being chosen bishop.

Musée Historique des Tissus, Lyons

PLATE X   Martin kissing a leper.

Musée Historique des Tissus, Lyons

PLATE XI Martin and the demoniac.

Musée Historique des Tissus, Lyons

PLATE XII   Martin and the proconsul Taedradius.

Musée Historique des Tissus, Lyons

PLATE XIII   Martin and the poor man.

Musée Historique des Tissus, Lyons

PLATE XIV   Martin and the archdeacon with a cloak.

Musée Historique des Tissus, Lyons

to get the man some garments, but the deacon "tarried over long," and so Martin entered the sacristy, took off his own tunic, and presented it to the beggar. When the archdeacon returned bringing with him a wretched robe intended for the beggar, Martin clad himself in it and went into the church. Voragine writes that "as he sang Mass a great light of fire descended upon his head. . . . Then were brought to him by miracle sleeves of gold . . . full of precious stones . . . which covered his arms." In the Lyons roundel, Martin, on confronting the poor man, turns to his archdeacon, commanding him to fetch the garments. Another roundel (PLATE XIV) may represent the archdeacon who "tarried over long," finally bringing the "vile coat" to Martin. There is considerable restoration in the area of the cloak in this embroidery, hence the difficulty in interpreting the scene.

Two other roundels in Lyons, one showing Martin going into church accompanied by a deacon (PLATE XV), the other showing him coming out of church to meet a group of people led by a deacon (PLATE XVI), are also difficult to interpret because neither appears to contain significant storytelling details. They could refer to any number of episodes in St. Martin's life as bishop. It would be pleasant to think that the deacon represented is the famous one named Brice. This Brice was a great trial to Martin, although he later became bishop of Tours and a saint. Gregory, in his *History of the Franks,* tells how "one day when a sick man was looking for the blessed Martin . . . he met Brice, at this time a deacon, in the square, and he said . . . 'Behold I am seeking the blessed man and I do not know where he is or what he is doing.' And Brice said: 'If you are seeking for that crazy person, look in the distance; there he is, staring at the sky in his usual fashion as if he were daft.' And when the poor man had seen him and got what he wanted, the blessed Martin said to the deacon: 'Well, Brice, I seem to you crazy, do I?' And when the latter in confusion at this denied he had said so, the saint replied: 'Were not my ears at your lips when you said this at a distance? Verily I say unto you that I have prevailed upon God that you shall succeed to the bishop's office after me. . . .' Brice on hearing this laughed and said: 'Did I not speak the truth that he uttered crazy words?'"[17]

Martin, as bishop, came into contact with two Roman emperors and their wives. It was at the dinner table of Emperor Maximian that Martin passed the wine cup first to his priest (PLATE XVII). The wife of Maximian was a

40

PLATE XV Martin with his deacon.

Musée Historique des Tissus, Lyons

PLATE XVI   Martin with his deacon and followers.

Musée Historique des Tissus, Lyons

PLATE XVII   Martin offering the wine cup to the priest.

Collection of Robert Lehman, New York

PLATE XVIII   The empress kneeling before Martin.

The Metropolitan Museum of Art, The Cloisters Collection, 47.101.63

devoted follower of Martin. According to Sulpicius Severus, "night and day the empress hung upon the lips of the saint." It seems probable that one of the Cloisters roundels (PLATE XVIII) represents the empress kneeling before the saint. Though she wears no crown, she is clad in a surcoat of ermine, the traditional garb of royal ladies. Sulpicius Severus says that "the empress never considered her imperial power, nor her rank in the empire, neither her diadem nor her purple; prostrate on the ground, she could not drag herself away from the feet of Martin." Sulpicius Severus says further that the empress at one time bathed the feet of Martin with her tears and dried them with her hair, and that this act greatly embarrassed the saint, "who never before had been touched by a woman."[18]

Other interpretations of the scene in this embroidery are possible. It may be that it was intended to represent Martin converting his mother to the Christian faith while his father remains adamant in his pagan beliefs. The chief objection to this interpretation is the age of Martin as he is shown here. According to all the accounts, the saint was a young man when he went over the mountains into Italy to convert his parents, and he is so depicted in the Cloisters roundel of his encounter with the brigands, which occurred, it will be recalled, on his journey to his home. In PLATE XVIII, however, the saint is surely a portly, middle-aged man. It may be said also that, in other known representations of the conversion of Martin's mother, the event is dramatized and made more explicit by showing the mother being baptized. Still another interpretation of this scene is possible. It could be the woman from Chartres begging Martin to bring back to life her dead child. However, in the many other representations of this episode, the child is invariably included in the composition. And so, it seems preferable to read this embroidery as the empress, wife of Emperor Maximian, kneeling at the feet of St. Martin.

Martin's relationship with Emperor Valentinian and his empress was not so friendly. According to Sulpicius Severus this emperor was a "fierce and haughty" man. Moreover, his wife "prevented him from showing to the bishop the respect that was his due." Hence when Martin tried to visit the emperor with certain requests he found the gates of the palace closed to him. After he had fasted seven days, Martin was instructed by an angel to go again to the palace, where all would be well. "So Martin went to the palace; the gates were open; no one stopped him, and at last he came into the presence of the emperor. That one saw him coming from afar, and gnashing his teeth demanded why he had been allowed to enter. He did not deign to rise before the bishop until his throne caught fire and that part of the emperor's body which had rested upon the throne started to burn. Thus the haughty prince . . . in spite of himself stood up before Martin." One of the Lyons roundels (PLATE XIX) illustrates this incident. A rather small emperor, accompanied by two courtiers, gazes at the flaming throne while Martin stands imperturbably by. Martin's biographer concludes the story by stating that "the emperor granted all Martin's requests because he acknowledged that he had felt the effects of divine power."[19]

Martin did much to extirpate paganism from Gaul. Once, after he had ordered a pagan temple destroyed, he saw the flames "brought with the wind to a house that was joining," writes Voragine. "And he mounted the house and set himself against the fire, and anon the flame returned against the might of the wind." One of the Lyons roundels (PLATE XX) shows Martin and his deacon confronting the burning house, commanding the flames to turn back. "And all things . . . obeyed this holy man," says Voragine.

According to Voragine: "There was a corpse in a chapel which was worshipped as a martyr, and St. Martin could find nothing of his life nor of his merits. He came one day to the sepulchre . . . and prayed unto our Lord that he would show to him what he was, and of what merit. And then he turned . . . on the left side, and saw there a right obscure and dark shadow. Then St. Martin conjured him, and demanded [of] him what he was. And he said . . . that he was a thief, and that for his wickedness was slain. Anon then St. Martin commanded that the altar should be destroyed." The destruction of the tomb of the false martyr is vividly shown in another of the Lyons roundels (PLATE XXI), with a "dark shadow" like a black devil hastily leaving his erstwhile abode.

Many beasts submitted to the will of Martin. Once, when some hounds were chasing a hare, Martin ordered them to stop, and so they did, writes Voragine, "like as they had been overcome." A roundel in Lyons illustrates this incident (PLATE XXII). St. Martin in a graceful contrapposto movement turns to face the "overcome" hounds while the hare leaps away unharmed on the left. At another time a hound barked at one of Martin's disciples. The disciple turned and said to the hound: "I command thee in the name of St.

PLATE XIX   The emperor and the burning chair.

Musée Historique des Tissus, Lyons

PLATE XX   Martin saving a house from burning.

Musée Historique des Tissus, Lyons

PLATE XXI   The destruction of the tomb of the false martyr.

Musée Historique des Tissus, Lyons

PLATE XXII   Martin saving a hare from hounds.

Musée Historique des Tissus, Lyons

PLATE XXIII   Martin and the barking hound.

Musée Historique des Tissus, Lyons

PLATE XXIV   Martin and the sheep being sheared.

Musée Historique des Tissus, Lyons

Martin that thou hold thy peace," and the hound was as "still as [if] his tongue had been cut off," according to Voragine. In a roundel in Lyons (PLATE XXIII), St. Martin, a deacon, and two "disciples" proceed on their way as the hound stops his barking. Another Lyons roundel (PLATE XXIV) shows Martin drawing a moral as he witnesses the shearing of a sheep. According to Voragine, the saint told his disciples: "This sheep hath accomplished the commandment of the gospel, for he had two coats, and hath given to him that had none, and thus . . . ye ought to do."

St. Martin lived to be over eighty years of age, and when he died, writes Voragine, his face "shone as [if] it had been glorified, and the voice of angels was heard singing by many that were there. . . . And as Severus, bishop of Cologne, on a Sunday after Matins visited and went about the holy places, the same hour that St. Martin departed out of this world, he heard the angels singing in heaven. Then he called his archdeacon and demanded if he heard anything, and he said: 'Nay'. And the bishop bade him to hearken diligently." Whereupon the archdeacon "said that he heard voices in heaven, to whom the bishop said: 'It is my lord St. Martin, which is departed out of this world, and the angels bear him now to heaven. . . .'. And the archdeacon marked the day and the hour, and knew verily after, that St. Martin passed out of this world that same time." A roundel in Lyons (PLATE XXV) depicts the deathbed scene, and the embroidery in the Walters Art Gallery (PLATE XXVI) shows the bishop of Cologne with his archdeacon and two other companions listening to the heavenly voices while the soul of St. Martin, wearing a miter and a halo, is tenderly conducted by angels to paradise.

Martin continued to perform miracles of healing and succor after his death. Several of these are among the Lyons roundels. In one (PLATE XXVII), he rescues a poor wretch who was hanged. According to Gregory of Tours, a man guilty of many robberies and other crimes was arrested and conducted to the gallows. He asked of his executioners only enough time to pray. With hands tied behind him, he threw himself on the ground and "began to invoke the name of the blessed Martin, in order to obtain from him pardon from his sins, if not help in his extreme necessity." As soon as he had finished his prayer, he was hanged by the soldiers and left for dead. "But when the soldiers were far away the ropes on his hands and feet fell away." He remained thus "suspended" for two days and was then discovered by a nun to be still alive. "It

PLATE XXV   The death of Martin.

Musée Historique des Tissus, Lyons

PLATE XXVII   The hanged man saved.

Musée Historique des Tissus, Lyons

PLATE XXVIII   The prisoners freed from jail.

Musée Historique des Tissus, Lyons

was the blessed Martin who rescued me from imminent death,"[20] said the thief to all who came to see the wonder. In the embroidery St. Martin is seen directing operations from the sky, surrounded by clouds; otherwise one would identify this scene with the miracle Martin performed while still on earth when he brought back to life another that was hanged.

On several occasions during his lifetime Martin had freed prisoners from jail. The Lyons roundel (PLATE XXVIII) showing two men with their feet in stocks and a third man about to walk out the door (his bonds are a later addition to the embroidery) may illustrate one of these incidents. Since St. Martin himself does not appear in the composition, however, it seems more probable that this scene represents one of the posthumous miracles. At one time, writes Gregory of Tours, "those who were detained in prison heard the chant of psalms and, admiring their sweetness, asked their guard what it was. He answered, 'They are carrying the relics of St. Martin and that is why they sing.' Then the prisoners invoked St. Martin, weeping, begging him to . . . deliver them from prison. The bars which restrained them broke, and their frightened guards took flight. The prisoners walked out free, and in the presence of all the people rendered thanks before the holy relics of the blessed Martin who had considered them worthy to be saved."[21]

The reliquary of St. Martin appears in two of the Lyons roundels. In one of them (PLATE XXIX), a richly dressed man with a cane or crutch under his arm prays kneeling before the shrine, while a solicitous companion tenderly touches him on the shoulder and another expresses awe and wonder with uplifted hands. This scene could illustrate almost any of a large number of miracles described by Gregory of Tours in which the lame, the paralytic, and the gouty were healed at St. Martin's tomb. It could conceivably represent Gregory himself, who was cured several times by virtue of St. Martin, on one occasion being delivered of a fishbone stuck in his throat.[22]

In the other roundel (PLATE XXX) the reliquary is shown in the background resting on trestles, and a crown is suspended from one of the carrying poles. In the foreground a table, very like an altar, is set up, spread with a white cloth on which are placed two cruets and three bundles of candles. A seated man presides over the whole; another man approaches. It would seem that candles and cruets of oil are being sold for offering at St. Martin's shrine. Candles ranked with gold and silver as gifts to the church of St. Martin, since

58

PLATE XXX   The reliquary of St. Martin on trestles.

Musée Historique des Tissus, Lyons

PLATE XXXI   The lame man and the blind man healed against their will.

Cooper Union Museum, New York, gift of Irwin Untermyer

PLATE XXXII Sunshine and rain on vineyards.

Musée Historique des Tissus, Lyons

Figure 9

Vintage scene with painting of St. Martin as patron of vintners over doorway at the left, from a manuscript of Petrus Crescentius.

Bibliothèque de l'Arsenal, Paris, ms. 5064, fol. 68 verso

candles were kept burning in perpetuity around the tomb. Pilgrims sometimes held lighted candles all night while praying for cures. Gregory of Tours tells of several miracles wrought by candles that were brought home as relics from the tomb. They appeased tempests, stopped raging fires, and healed the sick.[23] Oil offered at the shrine often miraculously multiplied, and oil from the tomb had marvelous healing powers.[24] The crown may be the one promised to the king of Galicia if he would contribute to the rebuilding of the church after one of the raids by the Northmen. Since the king of Galicia was content merely to send good wishes, he never received the crown.[25] The trestles and the carrying poles indicate that the reliquary is in transit. Thus the embroidery probably represents one of the many occasions on which the precious relics were removed hastily to a safe place as the Northmen came plundering the Loire Valley. It was during one of these journeys of the relics that the healing of the lame and the blind beggars (PLATE XXXI) took place against their wishes.

The last roundel to be discussed (PLATE XXXII) shows a fat man in rustic clothing tending grapevines while clouds spill rain on one side of him and the sun's rays stream down on the other. This embroidery reveals another of St. Martin's activities. He was the patron saint of vine-growers (*Figure 9*) and might be called upon to provide the right amounts of sunshine and moisture at the correct times to insure a good harvest. He was also invoked by wine-makers and tavern-keepers. The poet Péan Gastineau relates that Martin on one occasion during his lifetime turned water into wine,[26] and Gregory tells how he caused the wine to increase in flasks placed by pilgrims on his tomb. Martin's feast day, November 11, coincides in France with the fete of vintage, and a thirteenth-century proverb suggests the attendant festivities:

> *A la veille saint Martin,*
> *Toute vielle boit du vin.*[27]

ROUNDELS: STYLE

IN SEARCHING for parallels for the St. Martin roundels in other works of art, it was found that they most nearly approached the manuscript illustrations, paintings, and sculptures by French artists or by artists from the Lowlands who worked in France in the first third of the fifteenth century. The artists from the Low Countries were influenced by the courtly elegance of traditional French art while infusing it with fresh vitality. Their style has been termed Franco-Flemish, or, by purists, Franco-Netherlandish, since many of them come from other Lowland regions than Flanders.

The varying compositions within a circle recall the tondo paintings of the Franco-Flemish school at Dijon, Burgundy (*Figure 10*), and the circular border vignettes in books illuminated by the Bedford Master and his atelier (*Figures 11–17*). The Bedford Master had a flourishing workshop in Paris, where manuscripts were produced for such illustrious patrons as John, duke of Bedford, and his wife Anne, sister of Philip the Good of Burgundy, as well as Charles VII, king of France. Many of the circular vignettes in the manuscripts by the Bedford Master have abstract backgrounds as in the embroideries, several have checkered grounds, and others a suggestion of a naturalistic landscape with plants as in the roundel of St. Martin bidding his parents farewell (PLATE II). Buildings with round-arched doorways, introduced as stage-setting, are similar in the embroideries and the manuscripts. Similar, too, is the grouping of the actors in such scenes as a baptism, a deathbed, and a feast.

Many of the figures in the embroideries are slender and graceful in accordance with the Paris tradition. Other figures are stocky, some with fat bellies bulging above tight belts. Counterparts for all of these may be found in French or Franco-Flemish manuscripts, including those by the Bedford

Figure 10

The so-called "Small Round Pietà."

Musée du Louvre, Paris

Figures 11, 12

Border vignettes from a *Book of Hours,* workshop of the Bedford Master.

Austrian National Library, Vienna, ms. 1855, fols. 19 verso, 137 verso

Figure 13

Border vignette from a *Book of Hours* made for the duke of Bedford, workshop of the Bedford Master.

British Museum, London, Add. ms. 18850, fol. 120. Courtesy Trustees of the British Museum

Figures 14, 15, 16, 17

Border vignettes from a *Book of Hours,* workshop of the Bedford Master.

The Pierpont Morgan Library, New York, M 359, fols. 56, 163, 17, 88

Figure 18

Annunciation to the
Shepherds, from the
Rohan *Hours*.

Bibliothèque Nationale, Paris,
ms. lat. 9471, fol. 85 verso
(photo Bibliothèque Nationale)

Master, the Rohan Master (*Figure 18*), and the Limbourg brothers (*Figure 19*), and also in sculptures at Dijon made for the dukes of Burgundy. The attitudes of two of the figures in the embroidery of St. Martin informing his parents he will become a Christian (PLATE I) are very like those of two mourners on the tomb of Duke Philip the Bold in Dijon. The gesture of young Martin with his hand on his belt may be compared to *Pleurant* no. 34 (*Figure 20*); St. Martin's relative who expresses his sadness by cupping his chin in his hand is similar to *Pleurant* no. 29 (*Figure 21*). These tomb sculptures are the work of Claus Sluter of Haarlem and his nephew, Claus de Werve. The dead nude figure in the embroidery (PLATE VIII) is strikingly similar to the dead Christ in the Rohan *Hours* (*Figure 22*) and also the dead man in an illustration for the story of Job, by the Egerton Master, in a *Book of Hours* (*Figure 23*).

Figure 19 (OPPOSITE)

The Betrayal of Christ, from the *Belles Heures* by the Limbourg brothers.

The Metropolitan Museum of Art, The Cloisters Collection, 54.1.1, fol. 123 verso

Figure 20

Pleurant no. 34 from the tomb of Duke Philip the Bold of Burgundy.

Musée, Dijon

Figure 22 (BELOW)

Mourning over the body of Christ, from the Rohan *Hours*.

Bibliothèque Nationale, Paris, ms. lat. 9471, fol. 135 (photo Bibliothèque Nationale)

Figure 21

Pleurant no. 29 from the tomb of Duke Philip the Bold of Burgundy.

Musée, Dijon

Figure 23 (BELOW)

Job contemplating a dead man, from a fifteenth-century *Book of Hours*.

Formerly collection of H. P. Kraus

The garments of many of the figures are of lightweight materials hanging in supple folds in the traditional French manner, as is shown, for instance, in the Parisian *Parement* of Narbonne (*Figure 24*). The heavier but still supple robes of other figures and especially the ample cloaks draped in rich folds over one arm are reminiscent of those worn by the *Pleurants* (*Figure 25*), the Prophets on the "Well of Moses," and other sculptures of Burgundy. The treatment of belted tunics with little suggestion of the body beneath, as shown in the roundel of the baptism of Martin (PLATE IV), is very like that of the sculptured figure of an acolyte from the tomb of Philip the Bold (*Figure 26*). The pseudo-Kufic lettering bordering the slit in the gown worn by the kneeling man in PLATE VIII copies a similar sort of lettering in the round painting

Figure 24

Christ appearing to Mary Magdalene, detail of *Parement* of Narbonne.

Musée du Louvre, Paris

Figure 25

Pleurant no. 15 from the tomb of Duke Philip the Bold of Burgundy.

Musée, Dijon

of the Pietà (*Figure 10*). Conversely, the short brush strokes as highlights on the garment of one of the figures in the painting suggests the stitches in an embroidery.

Several of the faces in the embroideries are idealized, with delicate features, again in the traditional French style. Others are individualized, with definite personality. These reflect less manuscript illuminations than works of art on a larger scale, such as panel paintings, sculpture, or tapestries, where a broader treatment and greater characterization can be more easily achieved. For instance, the strong head of the standing figure in the roundel of St. Martin with the empress (PLATE XVIII) recalls the head of Christ from Sluter's "Well of Moses" (*Figure 27*) in Dijon. The faces of Martin, Hilaire,

Figure 26

Acolyte from the tomb of Duke Philip the Bold of Burgundy.

Musée, Dijon

Figure 27

Head of Christ from the "Well of Moses."

Musée Archéologique, Dijon

and the deacon in PLATE VI are strikingly similar to the bishop and deacon in the tapestry of St. Eleuthère (*Figure* 28), woven in Arras for the cathedral of Tournai. In a general way, several of the faces bear a family resemblance to those in paintings of the Franco-Flemish school at Dijon (*Figures 10, 29*). It is a pity that so few French and Franco-Flemish paintings of the period exist for comparison with the embroideries. But the paintings that do exist, together with the many manuscripts produced in France and the sculptures of Dijon, provide enough parallels to the embroideries to warrant the conclusion that the roundels are indeed Franco-Flemish, with a strong accent on the French.

It is evident that more than one artist drew the designs for the thirty-two roundels. Certainly the man who sketched the pattern for St. Martin and the brigands (PLATE VII) could not have been the same one who sketched Martin refusing to fight (PLATE V). The proportion of the figures is entirely

Figure 28

Bishop Eleuthère bringing to life the daughter of the tribune, detail of tapestry of St. Piat and St. Eleuthère.

Cathedral, Tournai. Copyright A.C.L., Brussels

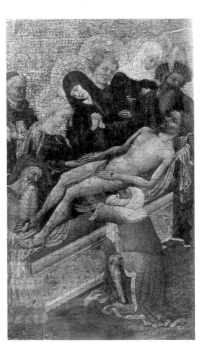

Figure 29

The Entombment of Christ.

Musée du Louvre, Paris

PLATE I   PLATE II   PLATE VI

PLATE VIII   PLATE XVIII   PLATE XXXI

different, the facial types are dissimilar, and, although St. Martin is wearing the same kind of garment in both embroideries, he could not easily be recognized as the same person. To be sure, some changes in the patterns may have been made by the embroiderers, but it is unlikely that these would be so extensive as to produce fundamental differences in style.

It is possible that as many as seven artists were engaged to illustrate the story of St. Martin. The work of one artist (*Figure 30*) is characterized by stocky figures with body forms evident beneath rather heavy silken garments, and bold and individualized faces with broad cheekbones, small chins, and well-defined eyes and eyebrows. Expressive hands play an important part in the action. This artist was especially inventive in arranging his characters to

Figure 30

Work of first artist

73

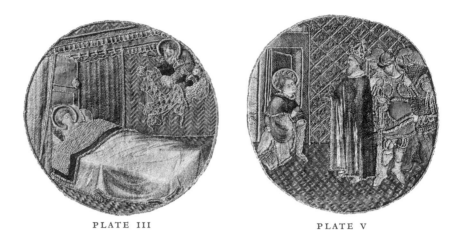

PLATE III   PLATE V

form varied and interesting compositions within a circle. His storytelling is superb. The best-preserved example of his work is the roundel of Martin and the empress. To the same artist may be ascribed the roundels of Martin informing his parents that he will become a Christian, Martin with Bishop Hilaire, and Martin bringing to life a dead man, the last noteworthy for its skillful depiction of a lifeless figure and face. In this group may also be placed the roundel of the spirit of St. Martin confronting the lame and blind men. Although much of the embroidery is missing, enough of the drawing remains to indicate a distinct relationship between the dead figure about to be brought to life and both the lame man with his useless limbs and clawlike hands and the blind man with his unseeing eyes. The imposing figure of St. Martin with his cloak draped over his arm is so like the emperor in the roundel of the saint

PLATE XIX   PLATE XXII

PLATE X

PLATE XIV

on horseback (the embroidery of the emperor's face is restored) that it may tentatively be placed in this group. In many ways the artist of this series seems to have been the most imaginative and distinguished of them all.

In sharp contrast to the roundels grouped above is the work of the second artist (*Figure 31*). His figures are taller and slimmer, and the faces are small with delicate features. The setting is almost as important in the composition as the characters in the story. This artist is responsible for the roundels of Martin dreaming of Christ, Martin refusing to fight, the prisoners freed, the reliquary of St. Martin in transit, and probably Martin kissing the leper, Martin receiving a cloak, and Martin saving the hare. In Martin receiving the cloak and Martin saving the hare, the artist has shown a strange interest in stumps of sawn off trees for a background. Largely because of similar, smaller

PLATE XXVII

PLATE XXVIII

PLATE XXX

Figure 32

Work of third artist

PLATE IV　　　　　　　　　　　PLATE XVII

Figure 33　　Work of fourth artist

PLATE XI　　　　　　　PLATE XV　　　　　　　PLATE XVI

PLATE XXI　　　　　　PLATE XXIII　　　　　　PLATE XXIV

stumps crowded into the composition of Martin bringing to life the man who was hanged, this roundel may be included in the group also. Again, the similarity of the figure of St. Martin with the hare to the figure of the emperor in the roundel of the burning chair suggests that the same artist drew both.

The embroideries of Martin's baptism and of his offering the cup of wine to the priest seem to be by a third artist (*Figure 32*). Both have suffered damage, especially in the faces, but there is an evident similarity in the tilt of the heads, the bloused and belted tunics, the figures lined up in rows, and the nearly symmetrical compositions.

A fourth artist drew several scenes of St. Martin as bishop wearing his cope and miter, usually accompanied by a deacon in dalmatic. In these roundels (*Figure 33*), St. Martin is a gentle, contemplative individual, and his deacon is wide-eyed and alert. There is little action, and what action there is seems to be in slow motion. Examples of this style are the embroideries of Martin with his deacon, Martin with the deacon and followers, Martin destroying the tomb of the false martyr, Martin and the barking dog, Martin and a sheep being sheared, and probably Martin healing the demoniac.

A more forceful Martin with heavier features and determined stance appears in the Lyons roundel of Martin and the poor man (*Figure 34*). This appears to be the work of still another artist, who is also responsible for the roundel of the bishop of Cologne hearing voices from heaven at the death of St. Martin. It is possible that the Cloisters roundel of St. Martin admonishing the brigands was also designed by this artist. The foreground with deep fis-

Figure 34

Work of fifth artist

PLATE VII   PLATE XIII   PLATE XXVI

sures in a barren soil is almost identical with that in the roundel of the bishop of Cologne, and the fat double-chinned face of the brigand pointing out the way is not very different from those of two of the clerics accompanying the bishop. The obvious differences in this case may be due to the work of different embroiderers.

Two fine roundels in good condition cannot be assigned to any of the groups so far defined, nor can they be assigned to the same artist. One illustrates St. Martin being chosen as bishop of Tours (PLATE IX). Here Martin seems to be a more worldly person than in the other embroideries. The faces of all the characters are individualized and remarkably expressive of their thoughts. Gestures are not important in the telling of the story. In the other, which shows pilgrims at St. Martin's tomb (PLATE XXIX), the faces of the pilgrims, hollow-eyed and solemn, express religious awe. The finely drawn hands contribute greatly to the mood. The artist who sketched the design for this roundel evidently enjoyed the drawing of ears.

The remaining roundels are either so badly worn or so considerably restored that there is little point in discussing their style; even tentative conclusions would be unwarranted.

At least half of the roundels are small masterpieces of the painter's art — as well as the embroiderer's — and the entire series is of major importance to the history of Franco-Flemish painting of the first third of the fifteenth century. The period is rich in manuscript illuminations, but extant panel paintings of the French and Franco-Flemish school are rare. Hence the embroideries, designed by Franco-Flemish artists, help to fill this gap.

ROUNDELS: TECHNIQUE

Highly Skilled embroiderers interpreted the designs provided by the painters. The backgrounds and foregrounds are worked in gold threads made by winding silver-gilt foil around a core of silk. These gold threads, known as *or de Chypre,* are laid on the surface of linen cloth and couched down with silks of different colors, sometimes in geometric patterns, at other times in the semblance of realistic settings. Two of the Lehman roundels (PLATES VIII, XVII) show in certain areas the original turning back of the gold thread at the outer edge of the circle. This is evidence that the embroideries were not cut down to any extent or reshaped when they were removed from their original setting. Besides the backgrounds, all of the buildings, many of the furnishings, costume details, and in certain roundels entire garments are also worked in laid-on gold. In addition to the gold, there is some work in silver, for details such as weapons and armor.

Some of the areas of gold show the beginning of the *or nué* (shaded gold) technique, often called Burgundian, because it was used extensively in vestments made for the Burgundian court. The golden robe of the gentleman on the left in the roundel of Martin leaving his parents (PLATE I) is a good example of *or nué* in its early development. Here the gold threads are laid diagonally on the surface of the cloth and held there by silk stitches, placed close together for shaded areas and farther apart for highlights. Darker and paler silks are also used, to accentuate the modeling. Prime examples of the fully realized *or nué* technique are the vestments made for the Burgundian Order of the Golden Fleece (*Figures 53, 70, 75, 76*).

Although there is a shimmer of gold throughout the St. Martin roundels, the rich gleam of silken threads predominates. The colors are mainly blue, red, and green, with touches of brown, flesh color, and white. The light blues are shaded with lilac, and the greens are vibrant, ranging from light greenish yellow to dark green-blue. The larger areas are worked mainly in split stitch, locks of hair generally in chain stitch, and borders of garments occasionally in cross stitch. The stitches in general follow the drawing lines of the figures, achieving an almost painted appearance, in contrast to the technique in the Flemish St. Catherine embroideries (*Figure* 35), where the stitches are mainly vertical and a more woven effect results. The method of stitching in the St. Martin roundels continues the tradition of the thirteenth and fourteenth centuries in France (*Figure* 36); that of the St. Catherine embroideries was introduced in the fifteenth. Future study may show that the French workshops continued the earlier technique well into the fifteenth century whereas the Flemish workshops adopted the newer technique somewhat earlier.

Figure 35

Incident in the life of St. Catherine. Embroidered roundel.

The Metropolitan Museum of Art, The Cloisters Collection, 47.101.61

Figure 36

Embroidered pouch, French,
14th century.

The Metropolitan Museum of
Art, gift of Mrs. Edward S.
Harkness, 27.48.2

Many of the roundels are badly worn, and two (PLATES XII, XX) have
been extensively restored. All of the Lyons group show unnecessary embellishments, presumably added in the seventeenth century when the roundels
were cut from their original settings and used on chasubles. The heavy out-
lines of halos, garments, buildings, and furnishings in this group, stitched
with coarse thread, stand out in high relief and detract from the subtlety of
the modeling of the original embroidery. That the Brummer embroideries
once had received similar "improvements" is evident from *Figures 5* and *6*.
These had been removed before Mr. Brummer acquired the embroideries in
1929.

ROUNDELS: DATE

LOUIS DE FARCY published the Lyons embroideries as dating from the fourteenth century;[28] Raymond Cox, in his catalogue of the Musée Historique des Tissus, labeled them sixteenth-century;[29] the more recent catalogues by Henri d'Hennezel call them fifteenth-century.[30] All three authors present these dates without comment.

I have arrived at the date of around 1430–1435 for the roundels chiefly from the comparison of their style with manuscripts, paintings, sculptures, and tapestries of the fifteenth century, and from a study of the costumes of the period as shown in works of art. The manuscripts, cited above in the section on style, date approximately between 1410 and 1435. Of the books by the Bedford Master and his atelier, the Bedford *Hours* in London dates from about 1423, the Vienna *Hours* about 1422–1425, and the Morgan Library *Hours* about 1430 to 1435. The Rohan *Hours* may be dated about 1418 to 1425; and the works of the Egerton Master in the early fifteenth century. The round paintings of the Dijon School have been dated about 1390 to 1410. The sculptured *Pleurants* on the tomb of Duke Philip the Bold were completed by 1411. The tapestry of the life of St. Eleuthère was given to the cathedral of Tournai in 1402.

The costumes, accessories, and hair styles in the roundels are consistent with this dating. To be sure, there are certain fourteenth-century survivals, such as the long hair of some of the men (PLATES VIII, X, XVIII), and more especially the coiffure of the kneeling empress in the Cloisters embroidery (PLATE XVIII). The arrangement of plaits of hair (sometimes false) hanging down both sides of the face, hiding the ears, was a mode favored by noble ladies of the last decades of the fourteenth century, as shown by the queen in the *Parement* of Narbonne (*Figure 37*). The empress's costume, consisting of a figure-molding, tight-sleeved *cotte* under a full-skirted surcoat attached to a low-necked plastron, was also in fashion especially in the fourteenth cen-

82

tury; however, it continued to be worn for ceremonial occasions well into the fifteenth. The gown of the empress in PLATE XVII would be considered more stylish by the elite of the fifteenth century. Called a *houppelande* in inventories, this type of garment was first worn by noblemen, from about 1360 on, and then became popular with noble ladies after Queen Isabeau of Bavaria chose such a robe for her entry into Paris in 1389. The *houppelande* of the empress in the embroidery, with its extremely long, ample sleeves, a collar that could be buttoned high under the chin or opened flat over the shoulders, and a wide golden belt drawn tight just under the breasts, is of the type seen in tapestries, tomb monuments, and manuscripts from about 1400 to 1435 (*Figure* 38).

Figure 38

Lady wearing a *houppelande,* from Boccaccio's *Des Cas des Nobles Hommes et Femmes,* made for Duke John the Fearless of Burgundy (died 1419).

Bibliothèque de l'Arsenal, Paris, ms. 5193, fol. 354 verso

Figure 37

Queen Jeanne de Bourbon, detail of *Parement* of Narbonne.

Musée du Louvre, Paris

Huntsmen from *Livre de la chasse* by Gaston Pheobus.

Bibliothèque Nationale, Paris, ms. fr. 616, fol. 13 (photo Bibliothèque Nationale)

Border vignette from a *Book of Hours,* workshop of the Bedford Master.

Austrian National Library, Vienna, ms. 1855, fol. 145 verso

The short outer garment worn by the young St. Martin and other youths in PLATES V, VII, and XVII is of the same style as that of huntsmen in the manuscript of Gaston Phoebus's *Livre de la chasse* (about 1405–1412) in the Bibliothèque Nationale (*Figure 39*), praying men in the Vienna *Hours* (*Figure 40*) by the Bedford Master and his atelier (about 1422–1425), and several other manuscripts dating from about 1410 to 1430. The distinctive features of this short robe are the full skirt reaching to below the knees and, more especially, the balloon sleeves closing at the wrists.

The *chaperon*, or hood, was a head-covering in use for hundreds of years; however, the arranging and draping of the *chaperons* to form hats with considerable flair was practiced mainly in the fifteenth century. The various ways of transforming the *chaperon* shown in the embroideries were especially stylish about 1430. The kneeling figure in PLATE XXIX wears an undraped *chaperon* that illustrates the essential parts of this type of headpiece (*Figure 41*). It consists of a hood (here thrown back), with a long queue (*cornette*) and a capelet (*guleron*) over the shoulders. The man selling candles (PLATE XXX) wears his chaperon drawn over his head under a hat, his face exposed by the opening, called a *visagière* (*Figure 42*). St. Martin in PLATE X carries his *chaperon* slung over his shoulder, the capelet swinging in folds (*Figure 43*). St. Martin leaving his parents (PLATE I) wears his *chaperon* with the *visagière* in a small padded roll around his head and the *guleron* hanging behind (*Figure 44*). Martin's father in the same roundel wears the *guleron* to

Figure 41

Detail of Plate XXIX

Figure 42

Detail of Plate XXX

Figure 43

Detail of Plate X

Figure 44

Detail of Plate I

Figure 45

Detail of Plate I

Figure 46

Detail of Plate VII

Figure 47

Detail of Plate XIII

Figure 50

Detail of Plate XIX

the side and a jewel on the front for decoration (*Figure 45*). In PLATE VII St. Martin has the queue and *guleron* tucked into the fold of the *visagière* (*Figure 46*). The layman in PLATE XIII has transformed his chaperon into an elaborate draped turban (*Figure 47*). Similar ways of wearing the hood may be seen in many manuscripts, for example, in the *Belles Heures* of the Limbourg brothers from the library of Jean, duke of Berry (before 1413) (*Figure 48*), and in border vignettes of the Vienna *Hours* by the Bedford Master and his atelier (*Figure 49*).

There is one *chaperon* in the embroideries with the *guleron* projecting forward (PLATE XIX, *Figure 50*). Although there is considerable restoration in the area, the new stitchery appears to follow the original drawing lines. This "forward" look in *chaperons* seems to have been particularly stylish from about 1400 to about 1420, to judge from the portrait in the Louvre of Louis II, duke of Anjou, probably painted between 1400 and 1415 (*Figure 51*), and the

Figure 48

The duke of Berry on a journey (detail), from the *Belles Heures* by the Limbourg brothers.

The Metropolitan Museum of Art, The Cloisters Collection, 54.1.1, fol. 223 verso

Figure 49

Border vignette from a *Book of Hours*, workshop of the Bedford Master.

Austrian National Library, Vienna, ms. 1855, fol. 103 verso

Figure 51

Louis II, duke of Anjou.

Musée du Louvre, Paris

presentation page of the *Livre des Merveilles* (*Figure 52*), made for John the Fearless, duke of Burgundy, who died in 1419, and many other manuscripts of the first two decades of the fifteenth century. From the evidence of the *chaperons* alone, the roundels might be placed toward the end of the "forward" look period, about 1420, and well before the 1440s, when the small padded circlet around the head became an extravagantly large *bourrelet,* and the queue was elongated to hang below the belt, fling around the neck like a scarf, or tie under the chin. Philip the Good, duke of Burgundy, and one of his courtiers wear *chaperons* of this later type in the presentation page of the *Chronicles* of Hainaut, painted about 1446 (*Figure 57*). This same manuscript page shows other later costume styles not present in the embroideries. Most important are the belts tight about the true waistline, the skirts well above the knees, the shoes excessively pointed, and especially, the sleeves heavily padded at the top to broaden the shoulder line.

All the costumes, secular and clerical, civilian and military, can be dated about 1425 or earlier. The same applies to swords and battle-axes, reliquary shrines and bishops' croziers. Although there is the possibility of some conservatism in the representation of saintly scenes, the evidence from the costume styles points to a date not later than 1435 for the series, with some of the roundels probably somewhat earlier.

A study of other surviving fifteenth-century embroideries is of little help in establishing a date for the roundels. In the first place, there are no embroideries so far discovered that are at all like these in style. In the second place, very few of the embroideries that are known are documented.

Among the embroideries that may be dated approximately is the sumptuous set of vestments in Vienna made for the Order of the Golden Fleece, founded by Philip the Good in 1430. This complete "chapel," consisting of an altar frontal and dorsal, a chasuble, two dalmatics, and three copes, is listed in the oldest inventory of the Order, dated 1477.[31] Unfortunately there are no items in the account books or inventories of the dukes of Burgundy that can be identified with these Golden Fleece vestments, and so there is no way of telling when they were begun, who drew the cartoons, or who stitched the designs with such sureness and finesse. Hence, as with the St. Martin roundels, scholars must resort to an examination of style and a comparison with

Figure 52

Presentation page, *Livre des Merveilles,* made for Duke John the Fearless of Burgundy.

Bibliothèque Nationale, Paris, ms. fr. 2810, fol. 226 (photo Bibliothèque Nationale)

226.

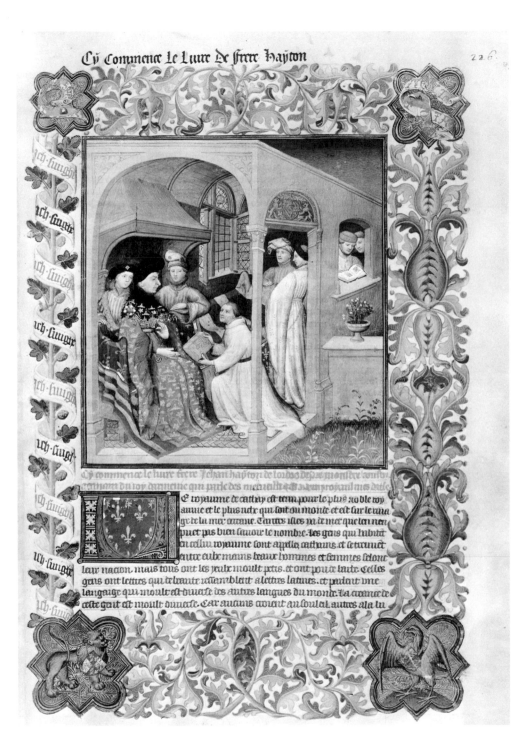

Cy commence le liure frere Jehan hayton de lordres des a monstre lomba cathain du roy dariene qui parle des merueilles et la en proiaul mes dele

E royaume de cattay est tenu pour le plus noble roy aume et le plus riche qui soit ou monde et est sur le rina ge te la mer oceane. Tantes isles in te mer que len nen puct pas bien sauour le nombre. Les gens qui habitt en cellui royaume sont appelle cathains et te trouuet uentre culer mains beaur hommes et femmes selonc leur nacion. mais tous ont les yeulr moult petis. et ont pour le tante celles gens ont lettres qui te beaute ressembleut a lettres latines. et parlent une langaige qui moult est duuerse tes autres langues du monde la crance te celte gent est moult duuerse. Car aucuns aroient au soul ael autres ala lu

other works of art to arrive at approximate dates and authorship for these vestments. It is generally agreed that the altarpieces, one of which is shown as *Figure 70* (detail *Figure 53*) are the earliest of the group, probably from the second quarter of the fifteenth century, and that all of these embroideries, early or late, are in the style of Bruges, Ghent, or Tournai.

The St. Martin roundels are quite dissimilar in workmanship as well as drawing style. The stitchery of the Golden Fleece embroideries is almost entirely in *or nué,* with only the flesh tones and a few details worked in shaded silks, whereas the roundels are mainly in different-colored silks with only a few details in *or nué.* The *or nué* of the Vienna vestments is extremely accomplished, almost machine-like in its precision; the technique could reach no greater heights. The *or nué* of the St. Martin embroideries is not only less extensive, it is also less developed. This fact, however, does not necessarily prove that the Martin roundels are earlier; it indicates merely that they were done in a different workshop. Although *or nué* was a fairly late development in the history of needle painting, it was not uncommon in France from the middle of the fourteenth century on. According to an inventory of 1352,[32] King John of France had a beaver hat trimmed with a band of embroidery presenting a picture, "true to life," of children playing on a flower-strewn ground and pigs eating acorns under an oak tree, all done in pearls, *or de Chypre,* and *or nué.* Thus the technique had been known and practiced long enough to have achieved perfection in the early decades of the fifteenth century.

The orphreys from a chasuble in the Petit Séminaire de Bonne of the Belgian village of Vellereille-lez-Brayeux may be dated within a twenty-three-year span by the coat of arms surmounted by a crozier that appears twice on the textile (*Figure 54*).[33] The arms are those of Jean Chevrot, bishop of Tournai from 1437 to 1460. One of the chief counselors of Duke Philip the Good of Burgundy, Jean Chevrot is shown in splendid scarlet robes with other members of the Duke's court in the dedication page of the *Chronicles* of Hainaut (*Figure 57*). Although the workmanship is less skilled than that of the roundels, there is at least one interesting similarity of technique. As in the St. Martin embroideries, the stitches in silk follow the direction of the drawing lines.

90

Figure 53

Detail, Golden Fleece altarpiece (Figure 70).

Figure 54

Detail of an orphrey from a chasuble.

Petit Séminaire de Bonne, Vellereille-lez-Brayeux, Belgium. Copyright A.C.L., Brussels

A very fine group of fifteenth-century embroideries from a cope, now in
the Historisches Museum in Berne (*Figures 55, 56*), included a coat of arms
once on the hood that may or may not have been added later.[34] The arms are
those of Jacob of Romont, duke of Savoy, who died in 1486. These embroideries, depicting the Seven Sacraments, are definitely later in style than the
St. Martin roundels, and they are purely Flemish in character.

Other embroideries with coats of arms or with written evidence for their
dates might be cited here, but, as said before, they are of little help in dating
the St. Martin roundels. It is to be hoped that some future study of embroideries will confirm the dates that have been established here chiefly by a comparison with other works of art and by the evidence of costume design.

PANELS:
ICONOGRAPHY

As has been mentioned, in addition to the roundels there are four exquisite embroideries in the shape of arched panels and one in the shape of an oval that apparently once formed part of this great ensemble devoted to the life and legend of St. Martin. These five embroideries differ significantly from the roundels in technique of stitchery and in style of drawing as well as in form; yet four of them were at one time in association with the roundels, and all of them illustrate unusual scenes of the legend, supplementing those of the roundels.

Two of the panel embroideries form the centers of the chasuble crosses at Lyons (*Figures 1, 2*). In one of them (PLATE XXXIII), St. Martin, a quiet, authoritative figure in a dark wine-red cloak, greets a visitor who is shown twice, first as he arrives at the saint's retreat and then as he kneels before his master. The landscape suggests a place of remoteness and solitude. This is probably Ligugé, outside Poitiers, where Martin founded a monastery before he became bishop; the saint in this scene is undoubtedly about to be persuaded by a stratagem to leave his cherished seclusion. As Sulpicius Severus tells the story, when the bishopric of Tours fell vacant, many citizens ardently desired that Martin be chosen to fill the vacancy, but it proved impossible to get him away from his monastery. "And so a certain Rusticus . . . pretended that his wife was very ill; he fell on his knees before the saint,"[35] begging him to come and succor her, and thus was Martin induced by a ruse to leave Ligugé. On the way, Rusticus and Martin were ambushed by hordes of citizens who conducted their prisoner under "good guard" to the city.

The second panel (PLATE XXXIV) illustrates one of St. Martin's many posthumous miracles. As told by Gregory of Tours, a man named Maurus "was stricken unto death and unable to speak." He made haste to take ship to visit St. Martin's basilica at Tours, hoping for a cure. As soon as he was on board,

PLATE XXXIII   Martin being persuaded by a ruse to leave Ligugé.

Musée Historique des Tissus, Lyons

PLATE XXXIV   Maurus cured on a boat bound for Tours.

Musée Historique des Tissus, Lyons

"the power of the saint restored his speech. Lifting his hands to heaven, he thanked God . . . saying 'even before having seen the temple of your saint I have been loaded with benefits.'"[36] In this brilliant embroidery the man in the bow of the boat, who has just been cured, lifts his hands in ecstasy, his face shining with joy. The wind whips his cloak and hair and the boatman's hat, and causes waves in the waters of the Loire. The basilica of St. Martin is visible on the far horizon.

The third panel (PLATE XXXV), in the collection of Countess Margit Batthyany, also once formed the center of a chasuble cross, as is shown in the 1887 photograph, in association with St. Martin roundels later in the Brummer collection (*Figure 5*). This panel illustrates one of the many miracles of healing the blind that occurred at St. Martin's tomb. The story of Bella as related by Gregory seems to coincide most nearly with the details of the embroidery. "A woman in the region of Tours, named Bella, had lost her sight and suffered much from her eyes. And she thought, 'If only I could be conducted to the basilica of seigneur Martin, I would recover my health, for I am full of confidence that he who by a kiss healed a poor man of leprosy would return the light to my eyes.' Then she went to the holy place with the help of a guide and there, persisting in fasts and in frequent prayers, she merited the recovery of the sight which she had lost. And she was so well cured that having arrived blind and conducted by others, she was able and happy in return to serve generously as a guide to the blind."[37] In the embroidery the poignant figure of the blind woman is tenderly "conducted by others" across a gangplank to shore; the same woman, now radiant, with seeing eyes, kneels in gratitude before St. Martin's shrine. The shrine in this panel is much more elaborate and more carefully wrought than the reliquaries shown in the roundels.

The fourth panel (PLATE XXXVI) must also originally have been a part of the ensemble of Martin embroideries, although until recently there was no direct evidence to prove it. The size, the shape, and the style of drawing definitely relate it to the other three. Also, once again, the subject adds a new incident to the story. Finally, the old photograph discovered by Mrs. Brummer in 1967 (*Figure 6*) shows this panel also as the center of a chasuble cross similar to the other three. As Voragine tells the tale illustrated in this embroidery, St. Martin was accustomed to ride upon an ass. "And horses that came

96

PLATE XXXV   The blind woman healed at Martin's tomb.

Collection of Countess Margit Batthyany, Castagnola, Switzerland

against him were afeard of him in such wise that they who rode on them fell down to earth. And then they took Martin and beat him grievously and he, saying nothing, suffered gladly the strokes, nor was not moved nor angry with them. And then they returned to their horses whom they found . . . fast to the ground, and they might no more move them than a rock till they returned to St. Martin and confessed their . . . trespass that they had done so by ignorance and prayed him to pardon them and to give them license to depart. And so he did, and then the beasts arose and went their way a good pace." Three scenes in the story are represented in the embroidery. In the background at the right the riders approach, at the left they beat St. Martin riding on his donkey, and in the foreground they beg his forgiveness while their horses remain immobile, their legs sunk in the ground, and Martin's amiable donkey watches the proceedings with interest.

Still another embroidery that belongs to the series has recently been discovered.[38] In its present form it is an oval, set like a jewel in an elaborate framework of gold braid and embroidery on the hood of a cope in the church of St. Michael in Ghent (PLATE XXXVII, *Figure 7*). In style of drawing and technique of stitchery, it is very close to the panel of St. Martin and the ass (PLATE XXXVI); indeed, the kneeling figure receiving coins in the foreground is almost a twin of the tormentor begging forgiveness. Moreover, the restorations, especially the distinctive rough-textured granular areas, are the same as those in the panel of St. Martin at Ligugé (PLATE XXXIII), and also in many of the Lyons roundels (PLATES III, XI, XV, XVI, and others). The beautiful gold patterns of flowers and leaves surrounding the embroidered scene on the cope are similar to the gold designs on the chasuble embroideries in Lyons, though more elaborate. The date 1561 on the gable of the barn at the right and also on the barn at left is stitched over restored areas and may record the year when this oval was re-embroidered.

Authorities in Ghent have maintained that the scene of the embroidery probably represents some incident in the life of St. Bavo, patron of the town.[39] Could this be verified, it would seem that the oval, in spite of its similarities to the St. Martin panels, was not, after all, a part of the ensemble. However,

PLATE XXXVI Martin and the ass.

Collection of Alastair Bradley Martin, Guennol, Long Island

a thorough search into the legend of St. Bavo has failed to turn up any incident that corresponds to the action in the embroidery. On the other hand, a story told about St. Martin, or rather, the power of St. Martin, related by Gregory of Tours, appears to fit the story in the embroidery neatly. It seems that the Frankish king, Charibert, following the example of his father, King Clothar, swore to the people of Tours that he would not impose taxes on them. Nevertheless, his lieutenant, Count Gaiso, began to exact tribute and went with the money that "he had collected to the king's presence. . . . But the king uttered a groan and fearing the power of St. Martin . . . sent back the gold coins that had been collected to the church of St. Martin, asserting that no one of the people of Tours should pay tribute."[40] In the embroidery a richly garbed gentleman, who may be Count Gaiso, is dropping coins in the hand of a messenger who has stabled his horse at the left. At the right the messenger leads out his horse for the journey to Tours, and, finally, in the background, he deposits the money into the outstretched hand of a custodian monk. The conclusion is that this oval originally formed part of the St. Martin series.

It is probable that this embroidery was originally of approximately the same shape and size as the four panels. There are additions on the sides of the oval, and it is obvious that there are missing areas at the bottom. In all subsequent discussion this embroidery will be referred to as a panel.

PLATE XXXVII   The tax money being returned to Tours.

Church of St. Michael, Ghent

101

PANELS:
STYLE, TECHNIQUE, DATE

Figure 57

Presentation page, *Chronicles* of Hainaut.

Bibliothèque Royale, Brussels, ms. 9242, fol. 1

Figure 58

The Visitation, by Rogier van der Weyden.

Speck von Sternberg Collection, Lützschena (near Leipzig)

Figure 59

Donors from the altarpiece of the Annunciation, by Robert Campin.

The Metropolitan Museum of Art, The Cloisters Collection

IN CONTRAST to the roundels, which show strong French influence, the panels are distinctively Flemish. The garments hang in stiff, tubular folds as in the presentation page of the *Chronicles* of Hainaut (*Figure 57*), which was probably designed by Rogier van der Weyden; or they fall in angular patterns as in a painting of the Visitation, also by Rogier (*Figure 58*). The treatment of the costumes of the kneeling figure at the left in the panel of St. Martin and the ass and the kneeling messenger in the embroidery of the tribute money returned is similar to that of the donor in the Annunciation altarpiece (*Figure 59*) by Robert Campin (the Master of Flémalle). The broad-brimmed furry hat of the messenger is in the same style as the straw hat

worn by Giovanni Arnolfini in the Betrothal by Jan van Eyck (*Figure 60*),
dated 1434, and that carried by the donor in the Annunciation altarpiece. The
figure of the blind Bella is very close to the Elizabeth in Rogier's Visitation.
Both wear gowns with the bodice fitting closely to the form, the skirt full, and
the sleeves tight, with furred cuffs. The blind woman's headdress, wide above
the ears, held out by small horns of hair, may be seen in many portraits, for
example, those of the donatrix in the Campin altarpiece and Jeanne Cenami
in Jan van Eyck's Betrothal.

The facial types in the panel embroideries may also be compared with those in Flemish paintings. The sad face of blind Bella as she is guided from the boat is very like that of Elizabeth in the Rogier's Visitation. The solicitous friend who guides her is not unlike the man in a drawing also by Rogier (*Figure 61*). The toothless old fellow begging forgiveness in the embroidery of Martin and the ass bears a family resemblance to Joseph in the Holy Family by Rogier (*Figure 62*); the same is true of Martin at Ligugé and St. Cosmos in the painting by Rogier of the Madonna with Four Saints (*Figure 63*). The expressive profile of the kneeling emissary to Martin in the latter embroidery is similar to that of the donor in the presentation page of the *Chronicles* of Hainaut.

Figure 62

Detail from the Holy Family, by Rogier van der Weyden.

Royal Chapel, Granada

Figure 63

Detail from the Madonna with Four Saints, by Rogier van der Weyden.

Städel Institute, Frankfurt am Main

Then, too, the greater emphasis on naturalistic settings reflects the love of landscape shown by Flemish artists, who so often open the window of a room to paint glimpses of a town or countryside. Although the sky in the embroideries is treated in an abstract manner with patterned gold, as befits a medium requiring richness as well as realism, and landscape details are kept to a minimum to avoid confusion, the treatment of trees and fields and swiftly flowing streams clearly displays a great desire to set forth the beauties of nature. A few examples of Flemish landscapes in paintings by Campin and

Figure 64

Detail from a Pietà, Rogier van der Weyden.

Royal Chapel, Granada

Figure 65

Detail from St. Luke making the portrait of the Virgin, by Rogier van der Weyden.

Museum of Fine Arts, Boston

Figure 66

Detail from the Visitation, by Rogier van der Weyden.

Speck von Sternberg Collection, Lützschena

Figure 67

Detail from Madonna in a Glory, by Robert Campin.

Musée Granet, Aix-en-Provence

Rogier are illustrated here (*Figures 64–67*) for comparison in a general way with the embroideries. Specifically, the wattle fence in Rogier's Visitation (*Figure 58*) may be compared to that in the panel of St. Martin at Ligugé.

There can be little doubt that these panels were designed by a Flemish artist of the highest ability and executed by embroiderers of extraordinary skill. When Martin Weinberger published the embroidery of the blind woman healed, he wrote: "From the drawing style, it seems to me not so far from the workshop of the late Rogier. The source remains in obscurity. . . . The subject is possibly a scene from a Tristan romance."[41] The source is no longer in complete obscurity, since it has been related to the St. Martin ensemble. Weinberger's opinion that this embroidery is not far from the workshop of Rogier van der Weyden seems wholly tenable, though it may be argued that this and the four other panels are closer to the earlier rather than the later works of Rogier. Judging from the style, it seems probable that all five panels were designed by the same artist.

In contrast to the roundels, where the stitches follow the lines of drawing, the stitches of the panel embroideries are mainly vertical. The stitchery is also much finer, rendering with exquisite deftness the drawings by the artist. The foregrounds of three of the panels (PLATES XXXIII, XXXVI, XXXVII) are stitched in silk instead of, as in the roundels, laid-on gold. Also, in the panel of Martin and the ass (PLATE XXXVI), a greater use is made of the developed *or nué* technique; the garments of St. Martin and his apologetic tormentors approach closely the work of the Golden Fleece embroideries.

Except for the panel of the tribute money returned, these embroideries have suffered comparatively little in the way of restoration. Most of the hands have been re-embroidered, but all the faces are in good condition. The two panels at Lyons and the one in Ghent have had embellishments added, especially on the borders of garments.

The panels appear to be somewhat later in date than the roundels, probably about 1440 to 1445. The paintings that seem closest to the panels date from about 1425 to about 1440; the manuscript page was designed about 1446. But the elaborate *bourrelet* and the exaggerated shoulders of the tunic worn by Philip the Good in the manuscript do not appear in the embroideries. All of the costumes, hats, and headdresses could have been worn about 1440. The technique of embroidery is consistent with this date.

PANELS:
DRAWINGS

Figure 68

Drawing after the embroidery of
the blind woman healed.
W. 6¼ in.
(See PLATE XXXV)

University Library, Uppsala

THERE ARE in existence numerous drawings after Flemish paintings,
but drawings after embroideries are unusual. It is therefore remarkable that
there are drawings after two of the St. Martin panels (*Figures 68, 69*). They
were first published in 1934, by Campbell Dodgson,[42] as Netherlandish, about
1440, because "the costumes, and particularly the men's coats and hats and
the headdresses of the women, are so reminiscent of the Flemish-Burgundian
fashions seen in the later pictures of Van Eyck and in other Netherlandish
works." In a supplementary note in 1937,[43] Dodgson, acting on the suggestion
of Dr. Feurstein of Donaueschingen, identified the subjects of the two drawings as miracles of St. Martin. He also noted the existence of the two embroideries almost identical with the drawings. Until the present study of the St.
Martin embroideries was undertaken, however, no one had suggested that
the two panels being discussed here formed part of the large ensemble. Dodgson, in the same note, mentioned Max J. Friedländer's opinion that the embroideries were "superior and anterior to the drawings."

I am in complete agreement with Dr. Friedländer. The drawings, although worthy of praise, are more rigid and less subtle than the embroideries. All the faces in the embroideries are more expressive of character and emotion. For instance, the blind woman healed, in the embroidery, is filled with an uplifting joy; in the drawing she is merely a woman in prayer. The face of the kneeling Martin with the ass is that of a visionary and a saint; the same could not be said of the face in the drawing. Details of costume are also treated with greater subtlety. The brim of the hat and the collar of the rower of the boat in the embroidery of the blind woman healed have an extra, very satisfying curve, absent in the drawing. The round window added to the chapel housing St. Martin's shrine is in a strange position in the drawing, the tree on the hill seems superfluous, the shrine itself is less convincing than in the embroidery, and the portion of the shore in the foreground seems rather like a lump of clay. The conclusion is that the drawings are indeed copies of the embroideries and not preparatory sketches for them. The date for the drawings remains problematical, but their mere existence indicates that the embroideries were greatly admired.

Figure 69

Drawing after the embroidery of **St. Martin** and the ass.
W 6⅜ in
(See PLATE XXXVI)

University Library, Uppsala

ENSEMBLE:
HOW USED

Figure 70

One of the altarpieces made for the Order of the Golden Fleece.

Schatzkammer, Kunsthistorisches Museum, Vienna

EVEN THOUGH the existing St. Martin series is a large one, the original set must have been larger still, since many well-known events in the legend are missing: notably the scene of Martin dividing his cloak with the beggar. It will probably never be known exactly how the embroideries were arranged or what kind of vestment or chapel furnishing they enriched. Louis de Farcy suggested that the Lyons group were originally *fronteaux,* that is, cloths to decorate the front of the altar and to hang above and behind it. This supposition seems reasonable. Fifteenth-century inventories and account books list innumerable such chapel furnishings, richly embroidered, and several exist today. Already mentioned, as superb examples, are the altarpieces for the chapel of the Order of the Golden Fleece (*Figure 70;* detail *Figure 53*). Because of their subject matter, two earlier *fronteaux* are of special interest:

Figure 71

Detail of altar frontal, 14th
century: an angel playing a
musical instrument; Martin
dividing his cloak; the baptism
of Martin; Martin ordained as
exorcist by St. Hilaire.

Musées Royaux d'Art et
d'Histoire, Brussels. Copyright
A.C.L., Brussels

Figure 72

Altar frontal, Icelandic, 13th
century: Martin dividing his
cloak; Christ appearing to
Martin in a dream; the
baptism of Martin; Martin
reviving a dead man; Martin
saving a hanged man; Martin
made bishop; Martin con-
fronting a poor man; Martin
giving the poor man his
garment; Martin reviving a
dead child; Martin casting out
a devil from a cow; Martin
commanding the birds; the
death of Martin.

Cluny Museum, Paris

one is of the fourteenth century, embroidered with nineteen scenes from the life and legend of St. Martin, made for the church of St. Martin in Liège (*Figure 71*);[44] the other is a thirteenth-century Icelandic altar hanging in the Cluny Museum, with twelve scenes from the story of St. Martin in the form of roundels (*Figure 72*). If the St. Martin embroideries under study here did indeed form *fronteaux* for an altar, then perhaps the roundels provided an allover pattern, as in the Cluny textile and in a fifteenth-century manuscript (*Figure 73*), or perhaps they were arranged in bands as in the illustration of an altar frontal in a fifteenth-century *Book of Hours* (*Figure 74*). The panels, set in frames of columns and arches, may have formed a dorsal, along with the important missing scenes of St. Martin dividing his cloak, and perhaps other missing scenes.

Figure 74

Scene showing altar frontal decorated with roundels in bands, from a *Book of Hours*.

University Library, Aberdeen, ms. 25, fol. 251 verso

Figure 73

Scene showing altar frontal decorated with roundels, from a *Book of Hours* made for the duke of Bedford, workshop of the Bedford Master.

British Museum, London, Add. ms. 18850, fol. 120. Courtesy Trustees of the British Museum

It is also possible that the embroideries originally decorated a liturgical vestment such as a chasuble, dalmatic, or cope. An inventory of Jean, duke of Berry, describes a group of vestments, "worked very richly . . . of which the embroidery of the chasuble is of the life of St. Denis . . . the dalmatic is embroidered with the life of St. Agnes; and two copes are embroidered, the one with the life of St. Louis of Marseilles and the other with the life of St. Louis of France."[45] Charles VII, king of France, as honorary canon of St. Hilaire of Poitiers, ordered a cope richly embroidered for him with scenes of the life of St. Hilaire.[46] If the St. Martin embroideries were intended for a liturgical vestment, then the roundels might have served as repeat designs over the surface of the garment, and the arched panels as sections of the orphreys (*Figures 75, 76*). If the vestment was a cope, the hood might well have been embroidered with the missing scene of St. Martin halving his cloak with the beggar. It is conceivable that the roundels and the arched panels were distributed over a whole set of matching vestments and cloths for the altar, that is, a "chapel." Whatever the case may be, I would prefer to imagine that the St. Martin embroideries, delicate and detailed as they are, were arranged on a reasonably flat surface, not obscured by folds, so that each storied roundel and panel could be "read," understood, and admired by all.

Figures 75, 76

Copes made for the Order of the
Golden Fleece.

Schatzkammer, Kunsthistorisches
Museum, Vienna

and his wife. For the same hospital in Beaune he also ordered thirty-one armorial tapestries for use on solemn feast days to screen the beds of the sick.

A second member of the Burgundian court notable for his wide interest in art was Jean Chevrot, bishop of Tournai from 1437 to 1460, who commissioned the embroidery for a chasuble now at Vellereille-lez-Brayeux, mentioned above (*Figure 54*). He also ordered illustrated manuscripts, one of which is the *City of God*, now in the Bibliothèque Royale of Brussels (mss. 9015–9016), and the Seven Sacraments altarpiece in Antwerp, designed by Rogier van der Weyden for the cathedral of Tournai.

There was also Toussaint Prier, chaplain to Philip the Bold, later almoner for Philip the Good, and canon of the cathedral of Tournai. He presented to his cathedral the set of tapestries depicting the histories of St. Piat and St. Eleuthère, which he had ordered woven in Arras in 1402 by Pierre Feré. There were many other art patrons in the Duke's court: Pierre Bladelin, the families of Croy and Lannoy, to mention a few. There were wealthy patricians in the Burgundian domain such as Jocodus Vydt, who commissioned the famous Ghent altarpiece, foreign diplomats and businessmen such as Giovanni Arnolfini, and corporations and religious confraternities, eager to engage artists in one métier or another.

It cannot be shown that Duke Philip the Good or any of the others here mentioned was especially devoted to St. Martin. To be sure, the Duke possessed in his fine library an illustrated manuscript entitled *Histoire de sainte Hélaine, mère de saint Martin de Tours*,[55] but this story has little if anything in common with the story as told in the embroideries or in any of the known sources for St. Martin. According to this tale, Hélène was the daughter of a Roman empress; she fled the court to escape the incestuous love of her father, went to England, where she married the English king, Henry, and had several children, of whom one was Martin and another, Brice, who became the father of St. Brice, St. Martin's deacon. Although the story elevates Martin to the ranks of the highest nobility as the grandson of a Roman empress and the son of an English king, and although the inclusion of Martin's name was obviously intended to lend credence to a fabulous narrative, there is no suggestion here of any real interest in St. Martin himself. Thus it cannot be said that because he possessed this manuscript, Philip the Good had a special personal veneration for St. Martin.

In the Duke's domain, however, there were many abbeys and churches dedicated to St. Martin, and any one of them might have been the recipient of an ensemble of St. Martin embroideries presented by the duke or by an affluent courtier. Again, one of the abbeys or churches may have commissioned the embroideries. Several of them were especially celebrated. There was the Abbey of St. Martin in Autun, Chancellor Rolin's home town, which was "enriched and protected by princes" and possessed in the Middle Ages about 30,000 "manses." There was the Abbey of St. Martin in Tournai, a center for manuscript illumination, which claimed one of the few relics of St. Martin outside of Tours, a tooth said to have been presented by St. Eloi. Interestingly enough, the reliquary in the panel of the blind woman healed (PLATE XXXV), with its seated figures separated by double colonnettes, resembles the reliquary of St. Eleuthère in the cathedral of Tournai (*Figure 77*),

Figure 77

Reliquary of St. Eleuthère, 13th century.

Cathedral, Tournai. Copyright A.C.L., Brussels

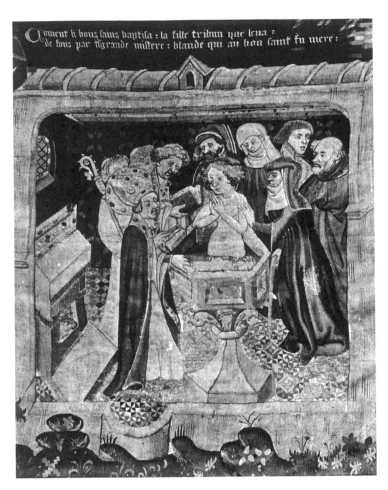

Figure 78

Baptism of the tribune's daughter by St. Eleuthère, detail of tapestry of St. Piat and St. Eleuthère.

Cathedral, Tournai. Copyright A.C.L., Brussels

Figures 79, 80, 81

Embroidered roundels: Martin dividing his cloak; Martin made bishop; Martin offering his wine cup to the priest.

Church of St. Martin, Courtrai

and the font in the roundel of the baptism of Martin (PLATE IV) is similar to the font depicted in the St. Eleuthère tapestry (*Figure 78*). There was the Church of St. Martin in Liège, which owned the embroidered frontal dating from the fourteenth century (*Figure 71*), and the Church of St. Martin at Courtrai, which at present possesses a dalmatic and tunic decorated with later, sixteenth-century roundels illustrating the life and miracles of St. Martin (*Figures 79–81*). Ghent also had a Church of St. Martin, and in Ypres both the cathedral and a monastery were dedicated to him. It was for the cathedral of Ypres that Nicholas van Maelbeke, abbot and also provost of the cathedral from 1429 to 1445, commissioned the last altarpiece to be composed and partially painted by Jan van Eyck. And then there was the city of Utrecht in the county of Holland, which was sometimes called Martinopolis because Martin was its patron saint. The cathedral was dedicated to St. Martin, and also an abbey and a hospice. The name and sometimes the figure of St. Martin was stamped on Utrecht's seals and coins, and the story of the saint was sculpted in bas-relief on the cloister walls in the fifteenth century. It is St. Martin who presents the bishop of Utrecht to the crucified Christ in a missal illuminated in Utrecht for Zweder of Culemberg, schismatic bishop from 1425 to 1453. Utrecht was indeed the city of the Burgundian realm most devoted to Martin.

It is conceivable, of course, that the St. Martin embroideries were donated by Philip the Good or a member of his court to one of the thousands of churches dedicated to St. Martin outside the Duke's domain. Perhaps they were intended for the greatest of all St. Martin shrines, that is, St. Martin of Tours. There is no indication in the records, however, that Philip or any one of the possible Burgundian patrons showed any interest in the basilica at Tours, even though the dukes of Burgundy, along with the dukes of Anjou and other peers of the realm, were by tradition honorary canons of the church.

René I (1409–1480), duke of Anjou, on the other hand, showed special veneration for the "glorious" St. Martin. A letter from the chapter at Tours thanked the "very excellent, very high, very powerful prince" for the devotion that he had always entertained for the saint, for the "graces, favors and goods" that he had bestowed on the church, and most specifically for the "ornaments and church vestments" he had brought to St. Martin's from the "country of Provence."[56] René, in fighting for his inheritance, the duchy of Lorraine, had been captured by the Burgundians in 1431 and was a prisoner of Duke Philip, off and on, until 1436. He would have appreciated the roundel of St. Martin freeing prisoners. An amateur painter himself, he valued the work of Flemish artists and, after being released by Philip, employed painters from Flanders as well as from his own provinces in France. In general, however, the period of his wealth and largesse is later than the period of these embroideries.

King Charles VII of France (1403–1461) was also a patron of St. Martin of Tours. As sovereign of France, he was honorary head of the monastery and was one of the French kings to be solemnly installed as abbot. In 1445 Charles contributed three hundred gold crowns toward the creation of a splendid new *chasse* for the relics of St. Martin, and his mistress, Agnes Sorel, donated an equal amount in her will. The reliquary, the work of Jean Lambert, goldsmith of Tours, was fashioned entirely of gold and vermeil, enriched with "topazes, sapphires, pearls and emeralds." It was completed in nine years, and in 1454 the relics of St. Martin were ceremoniously transferred to the elegant new shrine. The *chasse* was destroyed in 1562 by the Huguenots, who pillaged the church of its treasures and burned the relics of St. Martin.[57]

Charles VII therefore also comes under consideration as a possible donor of the set of embroideries. As mentioned before, he ordered a cope with scenes of the life of St. Hilaire, embroidered in "fine *or de Chypre* [with] all the tabernacles in gold and the figures in silk" from his special embroiderer, Colin Jolye.[58] The date, however, was 1454. As with René of Anjou, the important commissions of Charles VII were later than the period of the St. Martin embroideries. In the early years of his reign Charles was engaged in a life-and-death struggle with the English forces on his soil, who moreover were supported by the Duke of Burgundy; during this time the king's fortunes were at a low ebb.

It must be said further that, for the same reasons, the resources of St. Martin of Tours were also in a sorry state at this period, and therefore it is unlikely that the ecclesiastics of the basilica ordered and paid for the embroideries themselves.

It may be that the set of St. Martin embroideries was made, after all, not for a church dedicated to the saint but for an important person whose name was Martin. Such a person might have been Pope Martin V (1386–1431), who chose his papal name because he was elected on November 11, the feast

day of St. Martin. His coronation at the Council of Constance in 1417 virtu-
ally ended the Great Schism that had been so disastrous for Christendom. The
new pope, an Italian of the great Colonna family of Rome, was concerned
with many problems, including the wars between France and England and
between Burgundy and France. On November 27, 1430, he sent Cardinal
Albergati north to work for peace between Philip the Good and Charles VII,
recently crowned king at Reims. Before this, the records show, Philip the
Good had sent gifts to the pope in Rome. In 1423 he presented to the pope
six pieces of tapestry "made and worked very richly with many histories of
Our Lady." [59] In 1425 Philip contributed 1080 gold crowns toward the restoration of Roman churches that had suffered vandalism and neglect during the
Great Schism. [60] Philip had his agents in Rome and his ambassadors to the
papal court to further his interests. One of them received the large sum of
3925 livres in 1426 for having conducted "the process of the cause matri-
monial" between John, duke of Brabant, and Jacqueline, countess of Holland,
who had appealed to the pope to have her marriage annulled. [61] For reasons
too complicated to set down here, an annulment would have harmed Philip's
chances of acquiring the territories involved. Pope Martin ruled against
Jacqueline.

It is possible that Philip planned a more personal gift to the pope, and
ordered cloths for the holy father's altar embroidered with scenes from the
life and legend of his patron saint. It may be that the St. Martin embroideries
were begun for Pope Martin but after his death in 1431 were completed and
given to a church dedicated to St. Martin in the duke of Burgundy's domain.

Thus we return, full circle, to Duke Philip the Good as the most likely
donor of the embroideries. He had in his employ the French and Flemish
artists and embroideries capable of producing these exquisite works, and he
also had the resources to pay for them. Moreover, he possessed in his library
several manuscripts of the *Golden Legend* and others described merely as
Lives of the Saints that could well have provided source material for the de-
signers of the St. Martin story. In his *Mémoires,* Olivier de la Marche (1425–
1502) says of Philip the Good: "He died the wealthiest prince of his time; he
left four thousand écus of gold . . . seventy-two thousand marcs of silver in
tableware . . . rich tapestries, vessels of gold garnished with precious stones
. . . a library very large and very well bound . . . two millions of gold in furnish-

ings alone; he died the most generous and open-handed duke of his time."[62]

Although many questions remain unanswered concerning the St. Martin embroideries, it is hoped that this study will contribute to a much-needed history of French, Franco-Flemish, and Flemish needlework. And since the relationship between needlework and the other pictorial arts was very close in the Middle Ages, it may well be that the publication of these superb embroideries will also add a chapter or two to the story of painting and manuscript illumination in Flanders and France in the first half of the fifteenth century. Finally, this remarkably extensive series of embroidered illustrations enriches the written story of one of Christendom's most beloved saints, invoked by kings of France and heroes everywhere, by knights on horseback and workers in the vineyard, by travelers, innkeepers, and people who like to drink, and by cloth merchants, tailors, mendicants, and those who minister to the sick. St. Martin was admired for his heroism in successful confrontations with emperors, devils, brigands, and pagans, he was revered for his many miracles and his power over nature; above all, he was loved because on a cold winter night in Amiens, as a young soldier, he drew his sword, cut his cloak in two, and gave half of it to a poor beggar in the street, "for he had nothing else to give."

APPENDIX

HERE ARE summarized the known facts—and a few rumors—concerning the more recent history of the St. Martin embroideries.

The embroideries in Lyons, twenty-two roundels and two panels (PLATES III, V, IX-XVI, XIX-XXV, XXVII-XXX, XXXII-XXXIV), were acquired from the dealer Martel in 1909. Beyond this fact, nothing is known of their history.

In 1887 six of the other ten St. Martin roundels and the panel of the blind woman healed (PLATES I, II, IV, VII, XVII, XVIII, XXXV) were on the back of a chasuble that was shown in a loan exhibition of textiles held in Crefeld, Germany. This information was obtained from a photograph in the files of the Victoria and Albert Museum, labeled Crefeld Exhibition, 1887 (*Figure 5*). It is impossible to identify with certainty this vestment in the catalogue of the exhibition.[63] It is probable, however, that it is the chasuble of Item 24, described as "of the fifteenth century . . . of green silk damask . . . with pomegranate [design] . . . cross and strip embroidered with figures in colored silks and gold." The chasuble was lent by Clergyman-Counsellor Münzenberger, Frankfurt-am-Main, who also lent several other items to the exhibition.

The undated photograph recently discovered by Mrs. Brummer (*Figure 6*) shows a similar chasuble, which includes the panel of St. Martin and the ass (PLATE XXXVI), the roundel of St. Martin ordained exorcist (PLATE VI) and five St. Catherine roundels. One of the St. Catherine roundels had apparently been transferred from the chasuble shown in the 1887 Crefeld exhibition.

If it were not for this fact, it could be concluded that the chasubles in the two photographs were the two mentioned by Louis de Farcy in 1919 as being in the hands of the dealer Duponchel (page 10). As it is, it seems probable that one of the chasubles owned by Duponchel in 1919 is that shown in Mrs. Brummer's photo, and the other was a chasuble reconstructed sometime after 1887 with the embroideries shown in the Crefeld photo minus the St.

Catherine roundel. The presence of St. Catherine roundels along with the St. Martin roundels and panels indicates that two separate sets of altar fittings or liturgical vestments, one devoted to St. Catherine, the other to St. Martin, were probably in the same place in the seventeenth century when the roundels were removed from their original setting and converted into chasubles.

Sometime in the 1920s, it is said, at least some of the embroideries were in the collection of Marczell von Nemes in Munich, who offered them for sale to Philip Lehman. This information was given by a dealer to George Szabo, curator of the Lehman collection, but it cannot be authenticated.

It has also been rumored that some of the embroideries were in an auction sale at the Hôtel Drouot, Paris, in 1926 or 1927. An examination of the catalogues of the auction house for these years fails to yield definite information, although in the sale of June 14, 1926, there was a "strip of green velvet with embroideries representing the figure of a saint, a virgin, *rinceaux* etc."[64] and in the sale of June 24–25, 1927, there was a "chasuble of cloth. Orphrey with old embroidery representing saints."[65] The owners of the works of art in both these sales were anonymous; the buyers are now unknown.

It is a fact that in August 1929 ten St. Martin roundels were acquired by Joseph Brummer from the dealer Salvadori in Florence, along with the eight St. Catherine roundels. The roundels at that time had not only been removed from their seventeenth-century setting as chasuble orphreys, they had been relieved of most of their restorations and embellishments.

Of these ten St. Martin roundels, one (PLATE XXVI) was bought from Mr. Brummer by the Walters Art Gallery, Baltimore, in December 1929; two (PLATES IV, XXXI) were bought by Judge Irwin Untermyer in 1931 and presented to the Cooper Union Museum in 1962. The two Cloisters roundels (PLATES VII, XVIII) were acquired from the Brummer estate in 1947, and Alastair Bradley Martin acquired his (PLATE II) in 1948. The remaining four (PLATES I, VI, VIII, XVII) were bought by Robert Lehman in 1949.[66]

The panel of St. Martin and the ass (PLATE XXXVI) was owned by Arthur Sachs in 1930, in which year he lent it to the Metropolitan Museum, where it remained until 1935. In 1946 he sold it to Joseph Brummer, and in 1949 Mr. Martin bought it from the Brummer estate.[67]

The panel of the blind woman healed (PLATE XXXV) was in the collection of Baron Thyssen of Schloss Rohoncz, Lugano, Switzerland, in 1930; it was published in that year by Martin Weinberger.[68] It is now owned by the Baron's daughter, Countess Margit Batthyany.

So far, attempts to learn something of the history of the oval (PLATE XXXVII) have brought no results.

There is one further rumor, reported to me by a creditable witness as this study is about to go to press. It is that other embroideries of the St. Martin series exist, but that their anonymous owner does not wish them to be disclosed at the present time.

NOTES

1. Louis de Farcy, *La Broderie du XIe siècle jusqu'à nos jours,* Supplement 2, pl. 236, p. 165.

2. Jacobus da Voragine, *The Golden Legend or Lives of the Saints as Englished by William Caxton,* VI, p. 149.

3. *Ibid,* p. 144.

4. *Ibid.,* p. 157.

5. *Ibid,* pp. 142–143.

6. This work has been published in French translation by Paul Monceaux, as *Saint Martin: Récits de Sulpice Sévère,* Paris, 1926. All subsequent references to Severus cite this translation.

7. This work has been published in French translation by H. L. Bordier, as *Les livres des Miracles et autres opuscules de Georges Florent Grégoire, évêque de Tours* (Société de l'Histoire de France, no. 103), Paris, 1860. All subsequent references to Gregory's *Miracles* cite this translation.

8. This work has been partially published in English translation by Ernest Brehaut, as *History of the Franks,* New York, 1916. All subsequent references to Gregory's *History* cite this translation.

9. J.-P. Migne, ed., *Patrologia Latina,* CXXIX, col. 1036 ff.

10. *Ibid.,* CXXXIII, col. 815 ff.

11. Voragine, *op. cit.,* pp. 142–158. Page references will not be given hereafter.

12. *Vie de Monseigneur saint Martin,* Abbot J. J. Bourassé, ed., Tours, 1860.

13. Severus, p. 100.

14. *Ibid.,* pp. 109–110.

15. *Ibid.,* p. 126.

16. *Ibid.,* p. 125.

17. Gregory, *History,* p. 22.

18. Severus, pp. 233–235.

19. *Ibid.,* pp. 231–233.

20. Gregory, *Miracles,* p. 57.

21. *Ibid.,* p. 39.

22. *Ibid.,* p. 197.

23. *Ibid.,* pp. 13, 15, 97.

24. *Ibid.,* pp. 99, 119, 147, 227.

25. Lecoy de la Marche, *Saint Martin,* p. 472.

26. *Ibid.,* p. 607.

27. *Ibid.,* p. 607, n. 1.

28. Louis de Farcy, *op. cit.,* caption for pl. 236.

29. Raymond Cox, *Le Musée Historique des Tissus: Soieries et Broderies,* pl. 9.

30. Henri d'Hennezel, *Musée Historique des Tissus: Catalogue,* no. 236, pp. 76–77.

31. Julius von Schlosser, *Der Burgundische Paramentenschatz des Ordens vom Goldenen Vliesse,* p. 14.

32. Camille Enlart, *Manuel d'Archéologie Française, Vol. III: Le Costume,* p. 167.

33. *Flanders in the Fifteenth Century: Art and Civilization* (exhibition catalogue), no. 156, pp. 334–336.

34. Jacob Stammler, *Der Paramentenschatz im historischen Museum zu Bern,* pp. 87–98.

35. Severus, p. 112.

36. Gregory, *Miracles,* pp. 325–327.

37. *Ibid.,* pp. 53, 55.

38. This embroidery was brought to my attention by Colin Eisler of The Institute of Fine Arts of New York University, who has published it in his article "Two early Franco-Flemish Embroideries—suggestions for their settings," *The Burlington Magazine,* CIX (Oct. 1967), pp. 571–580.

39. *The Crypt of St. Bavo Cathedral in Ghent* (exhibition catalogue), no. 416, and information supplied with the photograph by the Institut Royal du Patrimoine Artistique, Brussels.

40. Gregory, *History,* pp. 220–221.

41. *Der Cicerone,* XXII (1930), p. 379.

42. *Old Master Drawings,* IX (Sept. 1934), pp. 32–33, pls. 33, 34.

43. *Ibid.,* XI (Mar. 1937), p. 71.

44. M(arguerite) Calberg, "L'Antependium de L'Eglise Saint-Martin à Liège," *Bulletin des Musées Royaux d'Art et d'Histoire,* Series 3, 17th year, Nos. 1–6 (1945), pp. 22–43.

45. Jules Guiffrey, *Inventaires de Jean, Duc de Berry,* II, no. 1283, pp. 156–157.

46. Louis de Farcy, *op. cit.,* Text, p. 78.

47. Le Comte (Alexandre) de Laborde, *Les Ducs de Bourgogne,* I, p. 206, no. 696.

48. *Ibid.,* I, p. 205, no. 694.

49. *Ibid.,* I, p. 277, no. 979.

50. *Ibid.,* I, p. 339, no. 1137.

51. *Ibid.,* I, p. 307, no. 1069.

52. *Ibid.,* II, p. 208, no. 4000.

53. *Ibid.,* II, p. 393, no. 4959.

54. *Ibid.,* II, p. 287, no. 4925.

55. Lecoy de la Marche, *op. cit.,* p. 81; L. M. J. Delaissé, *Medieval Miniatures from the Department of Manuscripts, the Royal Library of Belgium,* pp. 180–183.

56. Lecoy de la Marche, *op. cit.,* p. 393, n. 2.

57. *Ibid.,* pp. 420–423.

58. See note 46.

59. Le Comte (Alexandre) de Laborde, *op. cit.,* I, p. 196, no. 664.

60. *Ibid.,* I, p. 208, no. 701.

61. *Ibid.,* I, pp. 244–245, no. 827.

62. Olivier de la Marche, *Mémoires (Collection Complète des Mémoires relatifs à l'Histoire de France,* Vol. 10), p. 267.

63. *Ausstellung kirchlicher Kunstwebereien und Stickereien der Vergangenheit* (exhibition catalogue), Crefeld, 1887, p. 7.

64. *Objets d'Art Anciens, Tableaux Anciens . . . Sièges et Meubles Anciens . . . Etoffes Anciennes* (sale catalogue), Hôtel Drouot, Paris, 1926, p. 18.

65. *Catalogue des Tableaux Anciens, Objets d'Art et d'Ameublement . . . Etoffes, Tapisseries, Tapis* (sale catalogue), Hôtel Drouot, Paris, 1927, p. 27.

66. Parke-Bernet Galleries, Sale Catalogue of the Brummer Collection, April 23, 1949, no. 511, p. 129.

67. *Ibid.,* no. 512, p. 130.

68. *Der Cicerone,* XXII (1930), p. 379.

BIBLIOGRAPHY

ICONOGRAPHY

Medieval sources:

Fortunatus, "De Vita Sancti Martini," in J.-P. Migne, ed., *Patrologia Latina*, LXXXVIII, Paris, 1850

Péan Gastineau, *Vie de Monseigneur saint Martin*, Abbot J. J. Bourassé, ed., Tours, 1860

Gregory of Tours, *De virtutibus sancti Martini*, French translation by H. L. Bordier as *Les livres des Miracles et autres opuscles de Georges Florent Grégoire, évêque de Tours* (Société de l'Histoire de France, no. 103), Paris, 1860

Gregory of Tours, *Historia Francorum*, partially published in English translation by Ernest Brehaut as *History of the Franks*, New York, 1916

Paulin of Périgueux, "De Vita Sancti Martini," in J.-P. Migne, ed., *Patrologia Latina*, LXI, Paris, 1847

Pseudo-Herbernus, "Miracula beati Martini post reversionem," in J.-P. Migne, ed., *Patrologia Latina*, CXXIX, Paris, 1853

Pseudo-Odo, "De reversione beati Martini a Burgundia, Tractatus," in J.-P. Migne, ed., *Patrologia Latina*, CXXXIII, Paris, 1853

Sulpicius Severus, *Vita sancti Martini, Epistolae*, and *Dialogi*, French translation by Paul Monceaux as *Saint Martin: Récits de Sulpice Sévère*, Paris, 1926

Jacobus da Voragine, *The Golden Legend or Lives of the Saints as Englished by William Caxton*, London, 1900

Modern sources:

Lecoy de la Marche, *Saint Martin*, Tours, 1890

Henry Martin, *Saint Martin*, Paris (1917)

COMPARATIVE ARTS

Amsterdam, Rijksmuseum, *Bourgondische Pracht* (exhibition catalogue), Haarlem, 1951

André Blum and Philippe Lauer, *La Miniature Française au XVe et XVIe Siècles*, Paris and Brussels, 1930

Brussels, Bibliothèque Albert Ier, *La Librairie de Philippe le Bon* (exhibition catalogue), Brussels, 1967

A. W. Byvanck, *La Miniature dans les Pays-Bas Septentrionaux*, Paris, 1937

Henri David, *Claus Sluter*, Paris, 1951

L. M. J. Delaissé, *Medieval Miniatures from the Department of Manuscripts, the Royal Library of Belgium*, New York, 1965

Detroit Institute of Arts, *Flanders in the Fifteenth Century: Art and Civilization* (exhibition catalogue), Detroit, 1960

Comte Paul Durrieu, *La Miniature Flamande au temps de la cour de Bourgogne*, Brussels and Paris, 1921

Max J. Friedländer, *Die Altniederländische Malerei*, Vols. 1 and 2, Berlin, 1924

Camille Gaspar and Frédéric Lyna, *Philippe le Bon et ses Beaux Livres*, Brussels, 1944

Abbé V. Leroquais, *Les Bréviaires Manuscrits des Bibliothèques Publiques de France*, Paris, 1934

Abbé V. Leroquais, *Les Livres d'Heures Manuscrits de la Bibliothèque Nationale*, Paris, 1927

Stan Leurs, *Geschiedenis van de Vlaamsche Kunst*, Antwerp (1936)

Henry Martin, *Le Boccace de Jean sans Peur*, Brussels, 1911

Henry Martin, *Les Joyaux de l'Enluminure à la Bibliothèque Nationale*, Paris and Brussels, 1928

Henry Martin, *La Miniature Française du XIIIe au XVe siècle*, Paris and Brussels, 1923

Erwin Panofsky, *Early Netherlandish Painting*, Cambridge, Mass., 1953

A. E. Popham, *Drawings of the Early Flemish School*, London, 1926

Jean Porcher, *Medieval French Miniatures*, New York, 1959

Pierre Quarré, "Le Couple d'Enfants de Choeur du Tombeau de Jean sans Peur," *Bulletin Monumental*, CV (1947), 27–39

Grete Ring, *A Century of French Painting, 1400–1500*, London, 1949

Domien Roggen, *Les Chefs d'Oeuvre de Klaas Sluter, Vol. 1: Les Pleurants de Klaas Sluter à Dijon*, Antwerp, 1936

Paul Rolland, *Les Primitifs Tournaisiens,* Brussels and Paris, 1932

Charles Jacques Sterling, *Les Peintres du Moyen Age,* Paris, 1941

Tournai, *Les Tapisseries de la Cathédrale de Tournai,* Tournai, 1883

Baron Verhaegen, *De Oude Kerken van Gent,* Antwerp, 1938

Vienna, Kunsthistorisches Museum, *L'Art Européen vers 1400* (exhibition catalogue), Vienna, 1962

Le Chanoine J. Warichez, *La Cathédrale de Tournai,* 2 vols., Brussels, 1934

EMBROIDERIES AND LITURGICAL VESTMENTS

Mary (Symonds) Antrobus, *Needlework in Religion,* London and New York (1924)

Mary (Symonds) Antrobus and Louisa Preece, *Needlework through the Ages,* London, 1928

Joseph Braun, *Der Christliche Altar,* Munich, 1924

Joseph Braun, *Die Liturgische Gewandung im Occident und Orient,* Freiburg im Bresgau, 1907

M(arguerite) Calberg, "L'Antependium de l'Eglise Saint-Martin à Liège," *Bulletin des Musées Royaux d'Art et d'Histoire,* Series 3, 17th year, Nos. 1–6 (Jan.-Dec. 1945)

Raymond Cox, *Le Musée Historique des Tissus: Soieries et Broderies,* Paris (1914?)

Moriz Dreger, *Künstlerische Entwicklung der Weberei und Stickerei,* Vienna, 1904

Isabelle Errera, *Collection des Broderies Anciennes des Musées Royaux des Arts Décoratifs de Bruxelles* (catalogue), Brussels, 1905

Louis de Farcy, *La Broderie du XIe siècle jusqu'à nos jours,* Angers, Text, 1890; Supplement 1, 1900; Supplement 2, 1919

Hermann Fillitz, *Die Schatzkammer in Wien,* Vienna (1964)

Victor Gay, *Glossaire Archéologique du Moyen Age et de la Renaissance,* Paris, 1887

Henri d'Hennezel, *Musée Historique des Tissus: Catalogue,* Lyons, 1929

B(etty) Kurth, "Genres of European Pictorial Embroidery in the Middle Ages," *Ciba Review,* no. 50 (December 1945), 1798 ff.

Gaston Migeon, *Les Arts du Tissu,* Paris, 1929

Julius von Schlosser, *Der Burgundische Paramentenschatz des Ordens vom Goldenen Vliesse,* Vienna, 1912

Marie Schuette and Sigrid Müller-Christensen, *A Pictorial History of Embroidery,* New York (1964)

Jacob Stammler, *Der Paramentenschatz im historischen Museum zu Bern,* Berne, 1895

Martin Weinberger, "Sammlung Schloss Rohoncz: Plastik und Kunstgewerbe," *Der Cicerone,* XXII (1930), 377–379

COSTUME

Michèle Beaulieu and Jeanne Baylé, *Le Costume en Bourgogne de Philippe le Hardi à Charles le Téméraire,* Paris, 1956

Max von Boehn, *Modes and Manners,* Joan Joshua, trans., Vol. 1, London, 1932

Camille Enlart, *Manuel d'Archéologie Française, Vol. III: Le Costume,* Paris, 1916

Joan Evans, *Dress in Mediaeval France,* Oxford, 1952

Francis M. Kelly and Randolph Schwabe, *A Short History of Costume and Armour, Vol. I: 1066–1485,* London (1931)

M. Viollet-le-Duc, *Dictionnaire Raisonné du Mobilier Français, Septième Partie: Vêtements, Bijoux de Corps, etc.,* Vols. 3 and 4, Paris, 1872, 1873

RECORDS AND BACKGROUND HISTORY

Medieval sources:

J. Barrois, *Bibliothèque Protypographique, ou Librairies des Fils du Roi Jean,* Paris, 1830

Georges Chastellain, *Chronique* ("Oeuvres de Georges Chastellain publiées par M. le baron Kervyn de Lettenhove," Vols. 1–5), Brussels, 1863

Georges Doutrepont, *Librairie de Philippe le Bon,* 1420, Brussels, 1906

Jules Guiffrey, *Inventaires de Jean, Duc de Berry,* 2 vols., Paris, 1894, 1896

Le Comte (Alexandre) de Laborde, *Les Ducs de Bourgogne,* 3 vols., Paris, 1849, 1851, 1852

RECORDS AND
BACKGROUND HISTORY (continued)

Medieval sources:

Lecoy de la Marche, *Extraits des Comptes et Mémoriaux du Roi René,* Paris, 1873

Olivier de la Marche, *Mémoires* (M. Petitot, ed., *Collection Complète des Mémoires relatifs à l'Histoire de France,* Vols. 9 and 10), Paris, 1820

Enguerrand de Monstrelet, *Chronicles,* Thomas Johnes, trans., London, 1853

Modern sources:

(Amable Guillaume) Baron de Barante, *Histoire des Ducs de Bourgogne de la Maison de Valois, 1364–1477,* Vol. 5, Paris, 1839

Paul Bonenfant, *Philippe-le-Bon,* Brussels (1944)

Otto Cartellieri, *The Court of Burgundy,* London, 1929

Lucien Fourez, "L'Evêque Chevrot de Tournai et sa Cité de Dieu," *Revue Belge d'Archéologie et d'Histoire de l'Art.* XXIII (1954), 73–110

J(ohan) Huizinga, *The Waning of the Middle Ages,* London, 1927

Design by Peter Oldenburg
Composition by Finn Typographic Service
Color plates and printing by The Meriden Gravure Company
Binding by Russell-Rutter Company

First printing, 1968, 8000 copies